MW01280023

HAVE YOU HEARD
THE ONE ABOUT...............??

BOOK I

ALL RIGHTS RESERVED

COPYRIGHT 1996

This book may not be reproduced in whole or in part, by mimeograph or
any other means, without permission. For information, address:

Jokes,
P.O. Box 2372
Green Bay, WI 54306

ISBN 0-9654803-0-5

PRINTED IN THE UNITED STATES OF AMERICA
1996

Did you ever hear a good joke but couldn't remember it the next day? Now, you'll always have it handy. Easily accessed. Table of contents denotes categories: golf, salesmen, church, (yes, church), senior citizens, farming, genies, ethnic jokes, potpourri, passing gas, and reverse psychology. Something for everybody. These knee-slappers are clever, mischievous, hilarious, shocking, sexy,and exciting.
Examples:

The Tomcat Salesman
The Rabbi Hears Confession
The Laughing Kangaroo
The Joke's On Me
Emalina Brown
Oh My Prince, Please Save Me
The College of Logical Deduction
Funny Thing You Should Mention It

There are over 130 of the funniest jokes that you have never heard anywhere else, will tickle your funny bone, make you laugh, and at the same time make you feel good.

For Additional Copies Contact:
E-Mail - Jokes @ AOL Com.
Fax - 414-497-0391
Send cash, check, money order or credit card number to:
Jokes
P.O. Box 2372
Green Bay, WI 54306

THE IMPORTANCE OF HUMOR

A leading health magazine recently published an article that emphasized the importance of humor in each of our lives. The article stated that everyone should read at least one good joke a day for good health. Whether you read a joke, or somebody tells you one, is immaterial; humor not only makes you feel good, it is good for you.

Almost everybody would like to consider themselves good story tellers. However, telling jokes takes practice, preparation, knowledge of the material content, and enthusiasm. When there is a boxing match, the promoter has a series of "preliminaries" to prepare the audience for the main event. Before a comedian appears to give a performance, he has a number of practicing would-be comedians get the audience "warmed up" for the star. In other words, timing of the "big one" is all important. You don't simply weigh in with your best joke for a starter. Do what the professionals do; prepare your audience for the big event.

Pay attention to detail. Every successful operation depends on the participants being very aware of every detail that goes into the development of the project. A builder wouldn't think of leaving out a supporting wall; similarly every detail helps build the story to the topping off or crowning achievement. In a joke, it's the punch line.

Don't be too anxious to get to the punch line. Let your listeners savor the story and enjoy the building process. Many jokes are spoiled because the teller gives away the punch line before building up to the top of the tale. Anyone can blurt out a punch line, but the effect of the joke is lost when the complete story leading up to the punch line is missed.

THE ART OF TELLING JOKES

Telling jokes is somewhat of an acting process. Don't be afraid to be dramatic; your listeners will react positively. If you don't have enthusiam for what you are doing, your listeners can't be expected to be enthusiastic in their response either. The better prepared you are, the better you can relate the story in a positive light with enthusiasm.

Whether this book is used to read the jokes and enjoy them, or to use it as a framework for a comedian's role, the humor in the jokes contained herein will give much enjoyment. If you use it to be the life of the party, or simply to entertain your friends, practice various inflections of voice for effect and impact. Always try to imagine what the author of the joke was trying to convey.

There was no intent in publishing this book to suppress certain ethnic origins, or to cause any pain for any of the nationalities mentioned. Humor should never be intended to hurt anyone; humor should be intended for amusement and entertainment. We hope you find it so and enjoy it thoroughly.

TABLE OF CONTENTS

HAVE YOU HEARD THE ONE ABOUT.....????

There was not much to do in this little town; on Friday evenings the local comics honed their talents and entertained the tavern's customers.. They would gather at the antique saloon and take up their seats next to the old stove as it provided the only heat for the building. Like a herd of dairy cows that know their assigned stanchions, and always return to the same one, each member of the forum had his or her own cherished location in the circle.

The group consisted mainly of a witty Irish bachelor, a salty widow who had an eye on the bachelor, a retired Belgian farmer, a German seed salesman who often joined them in the evening, the town know-it-all who inherited everything he owned, but was well liked, and at times the pharmacist, the butcher, Ernie, the cannery fieldman,and occasionally the priest and the minister, who liked their whiskey each of whom had a great sense of huimor, would contribute a new joke. Then too, one of the characters in the town known for his cheating in golf was Snickering Sam. He was very forward and implanted himself in the group whether he was liked or not. One of the jokes that went around among his playing partners was that if Snickering Sam ever got a hole-in-one, he would write zero on his card. There was one rather short, muscular, little guy, who was especially crusty. His nickname was Billy Bugger. Nobody knew much about him. He had a high pitched squeaky voice, and when he started to tell a joke, it was apparent that he would get to finish it.

They all had one thing in common; gathering around the old stove made them comfortable and talkative. They had found long ago that they could not agree on religion or politics, so they took the neutral ground; they told jokes. Nobody ever took offense, regardless of the subject matter. Political correctness was definitely not an issue.

GOLF

ARE YOU MARRIED TO A GOLFER?

Ernie wanted to tell about the young couple who got married and spent a week on their honeymoon.

On Saturday morning, the groom got up and said to his bride, "Honey, I've got a confession to make. I'm a golf addict; I golf every weekend. All day Saturday and all day Sunday. I should have told you sooner, but I was was afraid you might not marry me."

She said, "That's OK, dear. I'm going to be gone all weekend also, and I've got a confession to make too. You see, I'm a hooker."

"No trouble at all," he said. "Just keep your head down, and your left arm straight."

GOLF IS No.1

Ernie just had to continue with this one. A man had been marooned on an island for ten years without seeing a human being. One day a mermaid appeared. She swam up close and asked him, "What would be the first thing you would ask for if you knew your wish would be granted?"

"Boy, would I ever love a martini," he gushed out. Whereupon she reached in the top of her suit, drew out a martini, and presented it to him. He relished the martini, and noticed she was unzippering the bra part of her suit.

She asked, "How long has it been since you've played around?"

He excitedly responded, "You don't have a set of golf clubs, in there, do you?"

"FATHER, GOLF MAKES ME SWEAR A LOT"

The priest said,"I've got one about golf and confession that I would like to throw in here."

A golfer went to see the priest in the confessional, and wanted to qualify his sins, so he told the priest, "I swear a lot, Father, and I know I shouldn't, but I golf and sometimes things go wrong. Like yesterday. I teed off and hooked my ball into the woods, so I swore"

"I can understand why you would swear," said the priest.

So the man went on. "Then when I tried to hit out of the woods, I hit a tree, and I swore again."

"Yes, yes, go on,"encouraged the good Father.

"Then I took my five iron, sliced it slightly, but just enough to put it in the sand trap, and I swore some more."

"You surely had a lot of frustration, which gave you occasion to swear."

The sinner went on to explain, "I finally hit a good shot out of the trap and landed about a foot from the pin. And then..."

The priest, an avid golfer himself, couldn't contain himself any longer. He jumped up, came out of the confessional, looked the man in the eye and asked, "You didn't miss that G— dammed putt?"

MAKE THE HOLE BIGGER

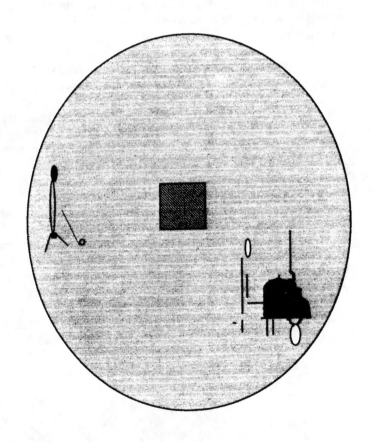

MAKE THE HOLE BIGGER!!!

The know-it-all was a pretty good story teller when it came to golf. He made Ernie the star of the joke as everybody there knew Ernie considered himself a real lady killer. Although not a very accomplished golfer, he looked for opportunities to play the game. On this particular day, he stopped at this golf course, and went out for a round. After a few holes, he caught up to a young girl playing alone and asked if he could join her. She had no objection.

She was an excellent golfer, playing slowly and deliberately. He played fast and was a hacker. When they teed up for the eighth hole, Ernie wanted to give her an incentive to play even better, so he said, ``If you par this hole, I'd like to take you out to dinner tonight. Besides, there should be some reward for being such a swell sport, like letting me play with you even though you're a lot better at this game.''

She said, "Thank you, Ernie. I'm enjoying your company, and since I am not doing anything tonite, I'll take you up on that. She parred the eighth and they proceeded to the ninth hole. Ernie was having an especially bad time, and finally got the ball on the green but just barely. It rested about 60' from the pin. She was feeling sorry for him and said, "You've been such a nice guy, inviting me out to dinner and all, that I thought I would give you an incentive to make your best effort. If you make that putt, you can stay the evening with me after dinner."

She knew he didn't have a prayer of making a long putt like that, but she thought it sounded generous of her.

This was a tremendous motivation. He held up his putter, lining up the route of the ball as he had seen her do. He had never made a putt over four feet in his whole life. He walked around and around, picking up every blade of grass, and anything else that might impede the ball in its path to the hole. He bent over the ball for the longest time; he stroked his club, looked back and forth, back and forth, finally he bent over, picked up the ball, and said, "This is a gimme if I ever saw one."

REVERSE

REVERSE

PSYCHOLOGY

PSYCHOLOGY

HOW EASY CAN IT GET

The salesman loved this story, because it had such an unexpected ending. This young executive was waiting for something to happen so he could become the top dog in the company. But events just were not moving fast enough for him. He was a little like the chauffeur for the famous scientist, who travelled widely, making an excellent income on the lecture circuit. After the chauffeur listened patiently for several years to the scientist repeating the same speech over and over, he asked the scientist, "I've heard this speech so often, I could deliver it for you. Let me do it."

"Why, that's preposterous," the scientist nervously replied.

"Not at all," said the chauffeur. "I know that speech just as well as you do, and I'm going to quit if you don't let me do it."

"What about questions at the end of the lecture?"

"They always ask the same dumb questions."

The scientist reluctantly agreed. On the appointed day, the scientist was sitting in the front row, nervously watching and listening. The speech went off like clock work. The chauffeur really had it memorized, but afterward, one of the listeners had a question that had never been asked before. The scientist cringed, wondering how the chauffeur would handle it. Amazingly, the scientist saw that the hauffeur was completely at ease.

He said, "You know, I've never had that question asked before. In fact, it's really kind of a dumb question. And just to show you how dumb it is, I'm going to ask my chauffeur, sitting here in the front row, to answer it for you!"

THE TABLES ARE TURNED, SMART ASS

The widow was rushing to get her turn. She wanted to tell the story about a woman who had just returned from attending her monthly club meeting. Her husband was already in bed, watching her as she undressed in front of the mirror. She told him, "The other women really liked the way I was dressed tonight, especially that sweater you bought me."

"They should have liked it for what it cost me," he replied.

"They liked the way I had my hair styled, too. And they thought my figure never looked better," she said as she strutted in front of the mirror.

"What did they say about your big ass?" he asked insultingly.

"Why, they never mentioned you at all, dear," she retorted.

I EAT LIKE A HORSE, DOCTOR

And then the salesman added this one for good measure. This man had been going from one doctor to another to seek relief. None of them were able to help him. He was telling his story for the umpteenth time. "I have a severe problem, Doc. I eat like a horse. It's awful. I can't stop eating. I eat all the time. This is really getting to me, Doc. The cost is driving me to the poorhouse. It takes a lot of time, the elimination problems are astronomical. I've been all over trying to get a cure, and nobody knows what to do........."

The doctor was listening and said nothing. But he was writing on his pad. The man that ate like a horse was impatient. He started to ask the doctor, "You know what to do for me? Boy, are you good! You're writing out a prescription already. Boy, am I happy I found somebody that can cure me. Give me the prescription, Doc..."

The doctor calmly replied, "This is not a prescription, my good man. It's a permit. This will allow you to keep shitting on the street until I figure out what's wrong with you!"

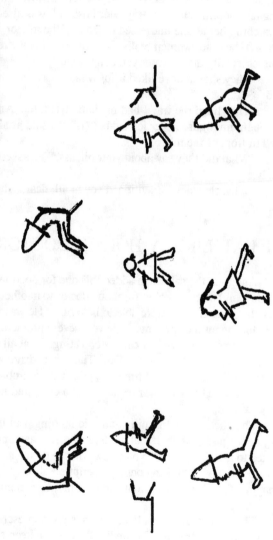

PEDRO & MANUEL

The butcher could really do the accent jobs. He loved to pretend he was Spanish and portray two Mexican lads, Pedro and Manuel, who had been drinking buddies for many years. One day, out of the clear blue sky, Pedro announces rather sadly to his good friend, that their good times are coming to an end. He almost cried as he said, "Me gonna get married."

Pedro's and Manuel's idea of a real good time was to drink and drink to find out who "champeen". Pedro said, "Tomorrow me gonna get married. Last chance to find out who "champeen."

As soon as the priest performed the marriage ceremony, Pedro was off to find his drinking buddy, Manuel. They trotted up to the bar and they drank, and they drank, and they drank. Pedro has reached his limit. He goes to sleep, and falls off the bar stool.

Pedro awakes with a start. He rubs his head. "What happen?" he asks himself.. He picks himself off the floor and slowly recalls the events of the day.

"Oh, boy," he says. "Me get married. Not see bride all day. She gonna be mad. Me bettter find her right now. Tell her I'm sorry. No more drinking with Manuel. No siree. No more drinking with Manuel from now on. But we had to find out one last time who champeen."

It's dark. He hunts all over the place, but can't find his bride. He finally gives up, and goes to his room, downhearted because he made such a fool of himself. He opens the door, and lo and behold, there is his drinking buddy, Manuel, in his bed with his bride.

His spirits pick up immediately. He laughs and exclaims, "Ho, ho, ho. Me champeen. Him so drunk, he think he is me!!!"

THE COLLEGE OF LOGICAL DEDUCTION

The know-it-all was the perfect guy to tell the joke about the professor at the **College of Logical Deduction.** One morning he bounded onto the stage of the study room and asked his class this question: "If I'm standing where Canada is north of me, the Pacific Ocean is west of me, the Atlantic Ocean is on my east, and Mexico is south of me, how old am I?"

The students were absolutely stunned! They all thought along the same lines. How can anyone, I mean anyone, come up with an answer to such a silly, silly, question?

But, lo and behold, one of the students yelled, "I've got the answer, Prof."

"Great," quipped the professor. "These are the kinds of problems you will be able to solve as you attend this great institution, the one and only, **College of Logical Deduction.** Now tell the class. How old am I?"

"44," the student replied.

"That's right. Good work. Now explain to the whole student body how you arrived at the solution."

"It was really quite simple. I've got a brother who's 22, and he's only half nuts!!!"

THE USED CAMEL LOT

Ernie had another rib-tickler ready. This businessman was taking a long trip in the desert, and since he had been advised that the best means of transportation was a camel, he decided to go to a used camel lot to buy one. {Camelot - said Ernie. Did you get that?

He looked at quite a few, kicked their legs, and told the manager he'd be gone for ten days. "Do you have any that'll go ten days without water?"

"No problem," said the salesman. "All our _male_ camels are guaranteed to go ten days without water. But you have to rock him before you leave."

The fellow put up the money, took the camel and was on his way. About seven days into the journey, the camel died. So he returned to the camel lot and asked for a refund. "After all, you guaranteed him."

The salesman was not too prompt in handing the money back to him. "Did you live up to the conditions? I told you he had to be rocked before you left."

"I did. I got alongside him and rocked him back and forth."

"But you see, if you had read the fine print, you'd know that's not the way to rock a camel. What that means is this: When he's at the trough for his last drink of water before you leave on your trip, you get two big stones, and while he's bending down, you smash the two stones together on his testicles. He sucks in his belly, and takes up enough water to last for ten days."

"But doesn't that hurt?" asked the novice.

"Not if you don't get your fingers between the stones!"

TAKE THAT, YOU BULLY

The butcher was a big strong fellow and identified well with this rib tickler he had in mind.

A rather small, very quiet gentleman frequented a bar in downtown Baltimore in which he felt perfectly comfortable. But one night a big muscular guy came in and sat down next to him. The big guy tried to get into a conversation by telling the little guy he had been a professional wrestler. Then he said, "Just let me show you a few holds."

The little guy wasn't sure what would happen if he resisted, so he went along with the idea. The burly wrestler grabbed the little guy's arms, twisted them behind his back, sort of locked them together, and proudly announced, "This comes from my long years of experience and it's called a crab bar." It made the little guy very uncomfortable, but he kept quiet.

The next night he took a different seat at the bar, hoping to avoid the wrestler, but to no avail. Soon the big guy was seated next to him, and wanted to give him another demonstration of his wrestling knowledge. This time the little guy said, "Never mind, I don't want to see anymore of your holds." But the wrestler would not be deterred. He grabbed the little fellow, took both his legs, crossed them, and put his head between his legs, so that it required two other people to release him. The big bully said, "This comes from my long number of years on the circuit, and it's called a crossing bar." This time the little guy was really upset, and left the tavern in a huff.

The next night the big wrestler came in and sat at the bar. Much later, the little guy entered the tavern very quietly carrying a package. He spotted the big brute and crept up behind him. When he got close, he unwrapped his package, and cracked the guy over the head, knocking him to the floor. He said, "When that big S.O.B. wakes up, you tell him that comes from my long years of experience shopping at Sears Roebuck and it's called a crow bar!!"

GREAT ADVICE

The salty widow went right on with this tale. There once was a guy who had fallen in love with another woman. As time progressed, he fantacized more and more and really wanted to have her all to himself. He felt his wife would not give him a divorce. Their sex life was good, but he wanted someone with more polish, which he felt the other woman had. He went to see his friend, the doctor.

After he revealed his problem, he asked, "Doc, tell me how I can get rid of her without committing a crime? Some way that's clean, no way for the law to check, painless. You know what I want. Help me out, doc."

"Well there's only one way to do that, my friend, without getting thrown in jail. Make passionate love to her. Morning, noon, and night. I can guarantee you that in six months she'll be dead."

The guy was strong and robust. He thrust his arm into the air and said, "Now why didn't I think of that?"

So the man left and since the doctor did not see her obituary in the paper or hear from his friend after almost six months, he took a ride out to his friend's farm to see him

When he rapped on the door, he heard a very weak voice from inside inviting him in. The doctor was not ready for what he saw. His friend was sitting in a chair, with a shawl around his shoulders, his feet in hot water, he had lost over fifty pounds, and presented a mere skeleton of the guy who had come to him for advice.

Dubiously, the doctor asked, "How are things going?"

"Oh fine, doc. Just fine," he whispered, for he was very frail and feeble.

"How's your wife doing and by the way, where is she?"

"Oh, she's out plowing in the back forty. The dammed fool doesn't know she has only a week to live."

SMART DOG

The elderly pharmacist always had a contribution to make. He went right ahead describing this episode.

A father sent his son to college, unaware of the cost involved. It didnn't take long, and the son wrote to his dad to send more money. Actually the son is having a great time with little devotion to his studies. After sending his son a considerable amount of money, the father says, "No more. I've had it. No more money."

He didn't hear from his son for awhile, but finally he gets a phone call, "You know, Dad, the college here recently opened a new department that teaches dogs to talk. I thought of you immediately, Dad. Your dog is exceptionally bright. You'd be able to carry on conversations with him. Wouldn't that be great?"

The father is tickled pink. "Why, I'd give anything if my dog could talk. He's the most faithful companion anyone ever had. How much would it cost?"

"It'll cost you a thousand, Dad. I'll see to it that the dog is taken care of and attends classes regularly."

"OK," says the father. "He'll be on the way in the morning and the check will be in the mail."

Six months pass and the son calls his father again. "That dog is not quite as smart as either of us gave him credit for. He will require special tutoring and extended lessons. I know it's not cheap, but we've gone this far, we might as well go the whole way. You'll have to send another thousand." The father reluctantly agrees. Soon

the second thousand is gone, and the son calls for more money. The father becames very angry and adamant that the son bring the dog home immediately so the father can check on his progress. The father is waiting patiently at the train depot for his son and the dog. The son disembarks minus the dog.

"Mother is waiting at home. She's eager to see you. But where's the dog?" the father anxiously asks his son.

"You know, Dad, that last thousand did the trick. With all that extra tutoring, he really came around. He was talking darn good. On the way home, we were having a conversation and he asked if Mother knows that you've been sleeping with the housekeeper every chance you get. I got so darned mad, I killed him right on the spot."

The father excitedly asked, "Are you sure he's dead?"

- 16 -

THERE'S NOTHING LIKE A GOOD MEAL

Ernie had thought of another one that he had to tell right away. This occurred in the old horse and buggy days, when a particular salesman was stranded at a farmhouse due to a snowstorm. The couple he stayed with, volunteered that he should sleep with them. They had only one bed so he had to sleep in the same bed with the husband and his wife.

In the middle of the night, the horses started to fight and made a lot of noise. The wife told her husband, "You had better get up, go out to the barn, and retie the horses."

When her husband got dressed and left the bedroom, she said to the salesman, "Now's your chance."

So he got up and finished the beans that were left over from supper.

BIRD WATCHING

Ernie had the floor and wasn't about to surrender it. "You know, I've been thinking of taking up a hobby for a long time. I found just the one that fits me to a "T".

His buddy knew him well. He never had a hobby in his life; he was too lazy. In fact, he was a confirmed couch potato. So he innocently inquired, "What hobby could you possibly be interested in?"

"I've taken up bird watching," he responded.

His buddy thought he would humor him. "What birds are you especially looking for?"

"Double breasted mattress threshers!!"

DO I KNOW YOU?

The seed salesman related the story of the couple who were taking a trip from Florida to California. The wife was hard of hearing. When the husband stopped at a gas station, the attendant asked where they were from. He told him and the wife asked, "What did he say?"

The husband obediently answered the question. Next, the attendant asked where they were going, and the man told him. Again, she could not hear, so she asked, "What did he say?" The husband patiently reiterated the conversation.

"Where are you from originally?" asked the station man.

"We were both born and raised in Detroit," he replied.

"Why, I was stationed right outside Detroit during the war. I dated a girl for quite some time while I was there. She was good looking, but not much in bed.," he laughed.

When the husband got back in the car to leave, she asked again, "What did he say?"

He responded, "He thinks he knows you."

A crowd was forming around the old stove and Ernie was responding to the attention. He could keep coming up with a new one. This he labelled,

SLIPS OF THE TONGUE

A lady boarded a bus in Milwaukee with three sets of triplets. The bus driver made a keen observation. "Triplets every time, eh?"

"Nah," she replied. "Lots of times we don't get any."

THE CASE OF THE PREGNANT GIRL

They were prepared to give the townspeople a good time. Ernie had this knee slapper ready.

A lady about seven months pregnant got on a bus and took a seat. She noticed a man sitting opposite from her smiling broadly, and feeling humiliated, she promptly changed to another seat, where upon the man's smile turned to a grin and he seemed even more amused. The lady moved for the second time, and the man burst out laughing. She complained to the bus driver and asked to have the man arrested.

When the case came up in court, the judge asked the man what he had to say for himself and he replied, "Your honor; it was like this. When the lady got on the bus, I couldn't help noticing her condition, and when she sat down under a sign that read, 'Gold Dust Twins Are Coming,' I had to smile. Then she moved under a sign which read, 'Use Sloan's Liniment To Reduce Swelling.' I couldn't keep from grinning. And when she moved the third time and sat below a sign reading, 'Goodyear Rubber Would Have Prevented This Accident,' I just laughed out loud.

"Case dismissed," said the judge.

THE MUCH MALIGNED SALESMAN

He leaves early in the morning full of energy and anticipation that he will make the "big sale". Today will be his day. His brief-case feels small and almost weight-less. He surely will surprise his boss, his wife, and even himself.

This is what many of his competitors see when they meet him in the cus-tomers' office. Unfortu-nately, some of his cus-tomers look at him the same way.

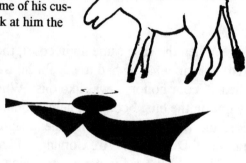

This is the way he views himself.

When he returns late in the day, his brief-case feels like it weighs a hundred pounds, his mis-sion has been a failure, and now he must motivate himself to do it over again the next day.

THE HURRY UP SALESMAN

The German seed salesman knew about this situation first hand. He told about another salesman who always over scheduled appointments; he was always in a big hurry. On one trip to a remote town in New Brunswick, it was necessary to fly in a propellor plane. On the way to their destination, the pilot announced, "We have lost one of our engines, and will be delayed about half an hour."

"Great," said the salesman. "Now I miss my appointment."

They flew on and again the pilot came on the address system, "Ladies and Gentlemen. There is no need to worry, but we have lost the second engine which will further delay our landing time by perhaps as much as an hour."

"Holy cow," said the upset salesman, "we're getting later and later. Now I'm going to miss two appointments."

But there was more trouble, as the captain made a third announcement. "We are sorry we are having so much difficulty. We have lost the third engine, but we can fly to our destination with one engine. We apologize for the long delay, which could be several hours."

The anxiety had overcome the salesman. He said to the guy in the next seat, "If we lose one more engine, we'll be up here all day."

THE EASTER BUNNY COMES BUT ONCE A YEAR

THE YOUNG WIDOW wanted to get this one off. A little boy came into the candy store before Easter and told the sales clerk that he wanted to buy a chocolate Easter bunny. "May I see one?" he asked.

He looked it over very carefully, and handed it back. "I would like to see another one," he said. The clerk handed him another one, which he looked over very carefully, turning it over and over. He handed it back and asked to see still another one.

After repeating this procedure three more times, the clerk queried him, "What is this all about?"

"I'm looking for a male chocolate rabbit," he answered.

She was perplexed. "Why a male chocolate rabbit?"

He answered indignantly, "There's just that much more chocolate in a male chocolate rabbit!!"

SHE THEN CONTINUED with this one for good measure. A young girl showed up for work on Monday morning with a black eye. Her friend asked, "Who gave you the black eye?"

She answered, "My husband."

"I thought he was gone for the weekend."

"So did I," she answered.

DIP, DIP, DIP, IN THE
NEW BLUE CHEER

ERNIE WENT RIGHT ON to tell about the door to door salesman selling New Blue Cheer. He had carefully worked up a routine to demonstrate to housewives how well the New Cheer would work. He asked to come in the house, set up a dish, put in some warm water, add the New Blue Cheer, and then take a wash cloth out of his bag and proceed to rinse it saying,

"Dip, dip, dip in the New Blue Cheer.
Dip, dip, dip, in the water clear.

Then he would remove it, squeeze dry it and continue with his song,

Run it past your nose
Smells like a rose.

Then he asked the housewife, if she would get something that she had to wash, so he could continue his demonstration. She was a sort of practical joker, so as she went to the laundry room to get something, she thought why not have a little fun with this, and brought her undies to him.

He blushed a little, then began,

"Dip, dip, dip, in the New Blue Cheer
Dip, dip, dip, in the water clear.
Run it past your nose
Smells like a ....
Dip, dip, dip, in the New Blue Cheer."

THE DOG FOOD COMPANY

The German seed salesman was a little philosophical and related the story of the dog food company, who held their annual meeting of sales personnel, to show them the last year's results and to encourage them to do better in the com-

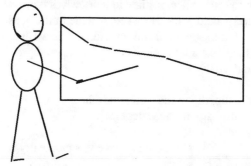

ing year. The manager was well prepared; he had brought many sales charts, graphs, pictures, and brochures to the meeting.

His promotion speech dwelled on all the perks he had supplied to the sales force, the visual aids the company provided, and introduced the support staff. But at the very end, he brought out his last and biggest chart. There was an undeniable downward trend in the line.

Sorrowfully and sadly he relayed to his salesmen that this represented the sales of the company. He asked one question, "How come, with all that we have done, the generous bonuses, all the other perks, our sales of dog food keep going down?"

There was an ominous silence. The sales force realized the manager had been extremely generous, yet the sales were not in proportion to his generosity. This was, indeed, a difficult point to ponder. "I ask you again. Does anyone have an answer as to why our sales are going down?"

It took a while before anyone responded. Finally from the back of the room, an old salesman gave them the answer. He said, "The dogs don't like our dog food!!!"

OH, FOR THE LIFE OF A TOMCAT

THE TOMCAT SALESMAN

The salesman was laughing, so this was their clue that they would have to listen to him.

HE WANTED TO TELL ABOUT this high classed salesman who was leaving for a convention in Toronto. A couple of days before he left, he informed his wife that he would need a costume. She had a hard time choosing the type of outfit to make, and finally decided he should go as a Tomcat. So she created a rather fine replica of a Tomcat, packed it in his suitcase, and he left for the convention. He was barely on his way, and she thought she would find out what really happened at these conventions, so she quickly sewed up a Pussycat costume, caught a plane for Toronto, and attended the affair.

By the time she arrived, the conventioneers were having their Costume Ball, and it wasn't long before she spotted her Tomcat. She sidled up to him and he asked her for a dance. After they danced for awhile, he suggested, "Why don't you come up to my room and spend the night with me. But only on one condition; we don't unmask. It'll be more romantic that way."

"Oh, that's just fine," she said. Not having to un-mask suited her fine, and they went to his room. The next morning she got up very early while he was still asleep, slipped out of his room, got to the airport, and flew home.

Somewhat later, her husband arrived home, looking very tired and weary. "Boy," he said, " that was a really rough convention. I got sick right after I got there, and I'm not over it yet. But don't worry about a thing, honey. Your costume did not go to waste. I loaned it to a friend and he said he had a ball."

NAN

The German seed salesman liked to poke fun at his own clan. He started the session on salesman jokes by telling them, "The German toastmaster always starts out the same way. He says, "Before I start talking, I want to say something."

There are a million stories about salesmen, but I really like this one. There was a salesman, who after checking into his hotel for the evening, got dressed to go out to eat. But first he decided to find out what was available in the bar room. There were two young girls seated alone at a table, so he casually walked up to them and said, "Hi, Nan."

She said, "My name isn't Nan."

"Oh, it isn't? I noticed the button on your lapel there spelled NAN."

"That doesn't stand for my name."

"What does it stand for anyway?"

"Actually," she said, "it stands for National Association of Nymphomaniacs. We're having our annual convention here now."

"Is that right?" he asked. His mind was racing. Boy, have I struck pay dirt this time. "I've often heard of nymphos, but I really always wanted to know one thing. What turns you on?"

"Anything having to do with Indians. Their colors, war paint, dress, tomahawks, tepees, whatever. Anything Indian."

He asked the girl seated next to her, "What turns you on?"

"Frenchmen. Anything French just drives me nuts. French cooking, you know their designs and all that, and the French accent." She almost wiggled right out of her dress.

"By the way," she said, "Let's get acquainted. What's your name?"

"Tonto LaRue," he blurted out in a French accent while giving a war whoop."

ANCHOR HIM DOWN

Snickering Sam came in and wanted his share of the spotlight also. He was in a bad mood this evening as he continued to criticize the company for which he was a salesman. "This new company I'm working for doesn't give a salesman much incentive to work," he said.

Ernie answered him, "You certainly have to get the right motivation to do a good job." Ernie admitted that Snickering Sam's situation was somewhat similar to the story of the warden at a prison who could not get the inmates to exercise. They needed an inducement, an incentive, some motivation so he got one of the local prostitutes to volunteer to run around the exercise yard in the nude in front of them. This really served its purpose well. He had the inmates running.

One day the State Superintendent of Prisons made a surprise visit to view the facility. Just as they were surveying the open central area, suddenly the prostitute ran out into the yard and all the inmates were running after her. "This is highly irregular," said the superintendent. "I demand an immediate explanation".

The warden apologeticalLy told him, "We just had to do something to satisfy the state's mandate for prisoners' exercise. The men refused to run or anything else, and the prostitute seemed to be a good solution."

"But," the superintendent asked, "why does that guy in the back have to carry that big pail of stones?"

"That's his handicap," replied the warden, "he caught her yesterday!!"

WRONG DECISION

The seed salesman told about his friend who had to spend the night with a farm family when his car broke down on a country road. The salesman explained his predicament and asked to stay overnight.

The father said, "We have only two bedrooms. So you have a choice; you can either sleep with the baby or sleep in the barn." The salesman wanted to be sure to get a good night's rest and didn't relish the idea of a baby crying all night, so he went out in the barn and slept in the hay loft.

When he arose the next morning, he walked through the stable where he saw a beautiful young girl milking the cows. She was startled, jumped up and he asked, "Who are you?"

She answered, "I'm the baby, but who in the world are you?"

Disgustedly he answered, "I'm the dam fool who slept in the barn."

NUTS!!!

THE GERMAN SEED SALESMAN liked to tell this true story about how he called on a customer who was eating his breakfast. He drank coffee with him and ate nuts that were on the table. When he finally completed the contract, he offered to replenish the nuts on his next visit.

The customer said, "That won't be necessary. Nobody in this family eats them anyway."

Impulsively, he asked the obvious question, "Why would you have a dish of nuts on the table if nobody eats them."

The man replied, "We only keep them there because the cat likes to lick the chocolate off the nuts!"

I CAN DO IT

Ernie said, "I've got to leave for awhile but I just thought you would like to hear about this young man who was having a hard time getting a job. He didn't have much confidence in himself and took a course in positive thinking. The instructor assured him it was very necessary to keep telling himself, **"I can do it."**

He read the want ads and discovered an advertisement for a job as a health insurance salesman. He applied immediately. At the interview, the sales manager gave him a rundown of the job, and asked, "Do you think you can handle that?"

"Oh yes," he replied. **"I can do it."**

"There's a girl called in here who wants a policy. Go out and get it." The sales manager gave him all the instructions but the young fellow was anxious to get going. The young fellow said, **"I can do it,"** and he was on his way. He soon returned with a policy application from a young girl, but he had neglected to get a urine speciman as he had been instructed.

"You'll have to go back. Can you get it?"

"I can do it," he said. "**I can do it.**" And he was off to secure the urine sample. When he returned, he had a pail in his hand, which he promptly set down at the manager's desk. He remarked, "I got the girl's urine sample."

"This whole pailful?" queried the manager.

"On my way back, I passed some offices, so I stopped and sold them a group policy."

DON'T FENCE ME IN

Ernie had a penchant for the short little tales. This was about a salesman attending a convention in Atlantic City. He had far too much to drink, and as he made his way from one bar to the next on the boardwalk, he fell down and could not get up. When a fellow salesman came to his aid, the drunk said, "Let me alone. I'll climb this fence if it takes all night."

How about the salesman who was always dressed to kill, with the magnetic personality? Everything he wore was charged!!

Two Plains Georgia salesmen were discussing the fact that the people had to elect Jimmy Carter president instead of Billy.

"Why is that?" asked one of them.

The other replied, "Billy could run the White House, but Jimmy couldn't run the gas station."

SAY YOUR PRAYERS

THE GERMAN SEED SALESMAN had yet another tale about a salesman who was stranded and had to spend the night at this country house. He was relegated to sleep with a young boy. At bed time, the young lad put on his pajamas, and knelt down on the side of the bed. The salesman was impressed and thought he didn't want to do anything that would make him appear antisocial, so he knelt down, and pretended to pray.

The young boy looked up and said, "I don't know what you 're doing, but the pot is over on this side."

THAT'LL TEACH YOU

The salesman had another one. Two salesmen were travelling together in Minnesota. One evening, a severe snow storm forced them to sleep at a farmhouse, which was owned by a widow.

A year later, the two salesmen met at the post office. One of the salesmen was reading a letter he had just received in the mail. He said, "When we stayed at that widow's home in Minnesota last year, you snuck in her bedroom and slept with her, right?"

The guy laughed merrily. "Yeah, that's right. And she wanted to get my name, so I left her your calling card. Ha, ha. Why do you ask?"

Soberly, he answered, "She died and willed me the farm."

TOUGH DECISION

THE PHARMACIST told about a young man who was new in town and asked the pharmacist what he had to offer for gifts in candy. The pharmacist showed him a one pound box of candy and said, "That'll cost you $3.50."

The young man said nothing, so the pharmacist showed him a two and one-half pound size. "That will cost you $5.00," he said. The young man did not respond, so he showed him a five pound box and told him, "That will set you back $15.00."

The pharmacist was a good salesman, so he offered to help the young man make a decision. He asked, "How can I help you decide?"

"Well," the young man replied, "I don't know which one I'll take until after I have this date. I am going out with this girl tonight, and I'll decide before I take her out again."

This was foreign to the pharmacist who gave his wife candy <u>before</u> he took her out on a date. "What's going to be the clincher?" he asked.

"If she is cool, I might give her the box for $3.50; if she is a good necker, I'll probably go for the $5.00 one; and if I score, which I hope to do, then I'll give her the $15.00 box."

At the end of the day, the pharmacist found his daughter waiting to tell him that she was bringing a new beau home for dinner. When they were all seated, the young girl's mother asked the guest to say a prayer. He began to pray, "I am so happy to be asked for dinner by this sweet girl to introduce me to her fine family. Thank you for this wonderful food, etc. etc." He went on and on .

When they left for a movie after dinner, she said to him, "You have a real talent. I didn't know you could pray so elequently."

He answered, "I didn't know that your father is the pharmacist in town, either."

CHURCH

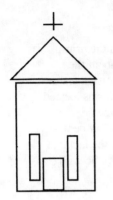

It was time for Ernie to spout off. He started by telling about an older man who met his friend at work on Monday morning sporting two black eyes.

"What in the world happened to you? How did you get two black eyes?"

"In church," he snapped back. It was plain to see he was quite unhappy.

"But how could you get two black eyes in church? That's where you go for peace and quiet, not fighting or anything like it."

"It was like this," the man explained. "There was this young lady sitting in the pew directly in front of me. When she stood up during the ceremony, her dress stuck in her crease, so I reached forward, and pulled it out for her. Bang. She hauls off and belts me in the eye."

"Serves you right. No woman wants a man to do something like that. That explains one black eye, but how did you happen to get the second one?"

"I thought as long as she was so upset because I pulled her dress out of her crease, I reached over and stuck it back again. That's when she turned around and gave me the second black eye."

COME AS YOU ARE

THE MINISTER popped in and chided the priest. "If you can tell'em, so can I." They let him tell about the priest who was having a hard time getting his parishoners to come to his Sunday morning services. His church was located in Florida near a lot of golf courses, and every time he brought up the subject they had a lot of excuses. But he noticed that most of the objections revolved around the fact that they did not like to get dressed to come to church.. So with that in mind, he posted a bulletin:

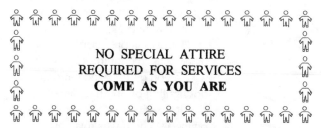

NO SPECIAL ATTIRE
REQUIRED FOR SERVICES
COME AS YOU ARE

The next Sunday, he stood at the entrance, greeting all his parishoners as they entered his church. He was tremendously pleased with the increase in numbers. Also near the church was a go-go dancers club. One of the girls wanted to attend the services, and since her routine ended just as ceremonies were about to begin, she made a mad dash to get to the church on time. There she was greeted by the priest, who promptly stopped her at the door.

"You are not allowed in church dressed like that, or I should say, undressed like that."

She pointed to the sign and told him rather sharply, "It says , COME AS YOU ARE. And besides that, as to attending church services, I have a heavenly right......"

He stopped her short, "You also have a heavenly left, but you still can't come in here."

A THERAPY SESSION

The priest knew that everybody, especially the non-catholics, seemed to get a kick out of jokes about confessions, so he threw this one in:

A man went to confession, and in the course of telling the priest his sins, he blurted out, "Father, I had intercourse three times last week." There was a momentary silence, and then the priest recovered, admonishing him for his unfaithfulness.

The priest said, "You know that's not right. You will have to atone for such an indiscretion."

The man protested, "But I wasn't unfaithful, Father. It was with my wife. Isn't it OK to have intercourse with your wife?"

"Why sure, " replied the priest. "That's not a sin. But why are you confessing that to me?"

"I had to tell somebody," he said.

THE RABBI HEARS CONFESSION

Much as people do in the confessional, the priest wanted to get this one off his chest. He began:

When the rabbi arrived to visit his good friend, the priest, they had only a short time before the priest had to hear confessions. The rabbi begged to leave, but the priest said, "This will only take a short time. There's plenty of room in the confessional, and that way we can visit between penitents."

"Well, OK, if you insist," answered the rabbi.

A man came in and begged forgiveness. "I know I haven't been the best man in the world; I fall into temptation. This week I had intercourse three times with the neighbor lady."

"For your penance, you go out and put $5 in the poorbox, and pray that the Lord forgives you."

Soon another man came in and he had a similar tale to tell. "I couldn't help myself, Father. I committed adultery three times this week."

"That's a serious sin. You go out, put $5 in the poorbox and say your prayers every day to resist any more temptation." The priest had a severe case of diarrhea, and told the rabbi to take over.

The rabbi was very apprehensive about this. "I've never heard confessions. What'll I do?"

"Just use your good judgment. You've heard the penance I've been passing out. Everything will turn out OK," he said as he left hurriedly.

The next man came into the confessional and told of his indiscretions. "I have sinned, Father, and I need forgiveness. Please help me. I committed adultery twice this week."

"You go put $5 in the poorbox, and then go have intercourse again with that same woman," said the rabbi. "We've got a special on this week; three times for $5.00!!"

PORK OR BEEF?

The minister was chuckling to himself. "What are you thinking about?" asked the bartender.

"Somebody told me this story and I think it's real cute," he answered.

Two men took their seats on a plane. One was wearing a collar and the other a skull cap. Since they were in the same profession, they had some guarded conversation. Not long after they took off, the flight attendant came and advised, "We have two entrees today for lunch. Pork or beef."

A little later she returned and asked the rabbi, "Have you made a selection?"

With a noticeable scowl in his voice he answered, "Beef, of course."

He felt it shouldn't have been necessary for her to ask. She then queried the priest and he replied,"Pork."

"Pork," snarled the rabbi. "I would rather commit adultery."

The priest retorted, "I didn't know I had a choice."

THE PRIEST AND HIS HOUSEKEEPER

The minister had a way of getting under the priest's skin, especially when he followed up with this little tale. A priest and his housekeeper had to attend some meetings in a distant city. When they checked in at a motel, they found there was only one room available. They called all over town, but couldn't come up with another room. It was getting late, so she said, "Let's take this one. We'll make do somehow."

They went to the room, she got ready for bed; luckily, there were two beds. She got in her bed, he used the bathroom and retired to his bed. Shortly, she said to him, "I'm cold. Could you please get me a blanket?" So dutifully, he got up, found a blanket, and covered her with it. A short time later she said, "I'm still cold." He was already dozing off to sleep and didn't answer her immediately.

Then she suggested, "Can't we play that husband and wife game?" He awoke long enough to answer, "Sure. But in that case, get up and get your own damn blanket."

HOW TO GET TO HEAVEN

The minister was on a roll. He told about three couples who were out for the evening when their car crashed. They all arrived at the Pearly Gates at the same time to be interviewed by St. Peter to be considered for entry into Heaven.

St. Peter said to the first man, "You certainly had a great desire to create wealth and accumulate money on earth. You loved money so much, that you even married a girl just because her name was Penny."

To the second man he said, "You were addicted to sweets on earth. You ate hugh quantities of sweets, got great big and heavy, which you know is a form of selfishness, and certainly the opposite of charity. You loved sweets so much, you married a girl called Candy."

The third man was listening attentively and said to his wife, "Let's get out of here. I'm sure we'll never make it anyway, Fanny."

THE TIME IS AT HAND

"By the way," said the priest, "we are taking up a collection for the addition to the school. And I want you all to be generous, or you will end up like the old miser who died and came to the Pearly Gates, and tried to enter into heaven.. St. Peter met him and said, "Not so fast. Before you can enter here, you have to prove your worthiness. What have you done on earth, that would allow you into my kingdom?"

The old fellow retorted, "Why, I was one of the richest men on earth. I could buy almost anything I wanted."

"You're forgetting that you had to leave your fortune behind, back on earth. That doesn't count here. Apparently, you didn't listen to the Church's Gospels, that told you to be generous and share your wealth with those less fortunate than you. The only thing that counts here, is how charitable you were on earth."

"I gave a waitress a dime for a tip once," he said proudly.

"Sounds pretty meager to me," said St. Peter. "Anything else?"

The old guy had really been a tightwad, and had to rack his brain to come up with any form of charity he had displayed. "Well, I put a nickel in the parking meter for a guy once."

"I don't know if you qualify. Wait here, while I talk this over with St. Benedict."

After hearing about the man's explanation, St. Benedict offered his advice, "Let's give him back his fifteen cents, and let him go to hell!!!"

CLANCY AND THE JUMPER

THE PRIEST continued as he liked to tell stories that had a religious connotation, like this one.

On the ledge of a tall apartment building, stood a crazed man, apparently ready to jump to his death. Firemen and policemen had arrived and tried in vain to talk the man down from his precarious perch.

"We'll have to call Clancy," remarked the policeman in charge. "He's our only hope."

Clancy was an old Irish cop with a thick broque you could cut with a knife, and had a very convincing manner. Many times he had been called in for situations just like this. They rushed him to the scene, as nobody in the department, could plead and coax like Clancy. He jumped out of the car, immediately grabbed the bullhorn, and in his inimitable style, began his patented routine, which was usually successful.

He called to the desperate man teetering on the very edge of his perch, "My good man, listen to me. If you won't think of yourself, think of your kids."

The man replied, "I don't have any kids."

"Well then, think of your parents."

Again the man replied, "My parents are dead."

Clancy would not give up. He got down on his hands and knees and continued to prevail upon him. In his best voice imploring and beseeching him as only Clancy could do, he yelled, "For God's sake then, man, think of the Virgin Mary."

The man thought a second or two and asked, "Who's the Virgin Mary?"

"You don't know the Virgin Mary? Jump, you S.O.B., jump!!"

ℓℓℓℓℓℓℓℓℓℓℓℓℓℓℓℓℓℓℓℓℓℓℓℓℓℓℓ
ℓ   The butcher thought this joke ℓ
ℓ applied here. He wanted to know if they ℓ
ℓ had heard about the guy from South ℓ
ℓ Dakota who thought "no kidding" meant ℓ
ℓ birth control?   ℓ
ℓ   ℓ
ℓℓℓℓℓℓℓℓℓℓℓℓℓℓℓℓℓℓℓℓℓℓℓℓℓℓℓ

PASS THE COLLECTION PLATE

The Priest wanted back in to tell about the prostitute who went to attend church services one Sunday, and when the collection plate was passed, she threw in a $100 bill. This did not go unnoticed by the minister, as he stood before the congregation and announced, "We have a very generous contributor here this morning. Would the person who contributed the $100 bill please stand up and be recognized?" Whereupon the young prostitute arose to a great ovation.

"As a special acknowledgement for your charity, you will be afforded the opportunity to choose the hymns for this morning's services," he said.

She looked about the church and pointed, saying, "I'll take him, and him, and him...."

FUNNY THING YOU
SHOULD MENTION IT

This was one of Snickering Sam's favorite jokes and he just had to tell it.

Abie and Ikie had been friends but hadn't seen each other for awhile. So when they met on the street one day, it was an occasion to find out how each had fared. In the truest Jewish tradition, they practiced the fine art of one-up-manship.

"Why, Abie, how good to see you after all these years. How are things with you anyway?"

Abie said, "Everything is just fine, just fine. And how is your family?"

"Funny thing you should mention it," answered Ikie. You know I had only one son, Abraham. In fact he has just completed college. Got his degree from Yale. And what about your son?"

Ikie couldn't wait to get his two cents' worth in. "Funny thing you should mention it. My son, Issac, just graduated from the finest Rabbinical College in the East. By the way, what is your son doing now?"

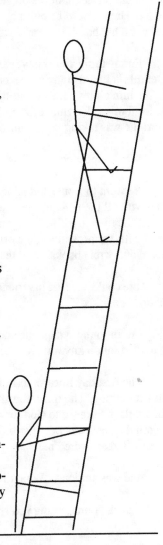

"Abraham was offered a job as Rabbi of the biggest synagogue in the city. Did your boy get a job yet?"

"Funny thing you should mention it. My Isaac is going to be the president of the biggest fabric mill in town. Quite a job. Ha,ha. He'll be pulling the wool over a lot of peoples' eyes, ha, ha. Has your Abraham gone to work yet?"

"Funny thing you should mention it. I thought that after all that hard studying he did for five years, I would give him a present, so I sent him on a trip to tour Europe for four weeks. But at the end of four weeks, he sent word, he was taking more time off."

"What happened then?" asked Abie.

"He went to Rome and joined a hippie crowd, associating with all the riff-raff. Said he had to find himself. Had to feel the ministry if he was going to be a good rabbi. He mixed with the prostitutes, the prisoners,talked with the fishermen, and wrote books," and then he paused.

Abie could see that his friend was grieved. "What did you do?" he asked.

"I went to the synagogue and prayed. Every day I prayed to God for an answer. "My God, I said, "What do I do?"

"The first day I heard nothing. And the second day I heard nothing. The third, fourth, and fifth day, nothing. For six days I prayed to God for an answer. Finally, on the seventh day, as I was praying to God, a bright light shown, and God answered me."

Abie was anxious. "What did God say?"

He said, "Funny thing you should mention it!!!

- 46 -

THE MEANING OF EASTER

The Lutheran minister was not bashful about
throwing in his versions of church jokes.

Three Polish men all came to the Pearly
Gates at the same time. St. Peter said, "Before I can
let you in my heavenly kingdom, you must be able to
answer one question. correctly . What is the meaning
of Easter?"

The first guy was ready to give an explanation. "That's the time when a star appears in the sky,
the Three Wise Men follow it, and find Baby Jesus
born in a stable."

"You're mixed up a bit there, my good man,"
said St. Peter. "You'll have to stand aside until you
get it right." He asked the second man, "What do you
think is the meaning of Easter?"

The second man went off on his explanation,
"All the people of the neighborhood get together and
have a big turkey roasting in the oven and everybody
has a wonderful time celebrating their good fortune.
They eat pumpkin pie with whipped cream, stuffing,
sweet potatoes, and they all have a very pleasant
time."

St. Peter grinned and said, "No. I'm afraid
that's not right." He wondered where they had gone to
school. So he asked the third Polish man, "What is the
meaning of Easter?"

"That's the time when Jesus was put through
hell on earth. They scourged Him, crowned Him with
thorns," and St. Peter was shaking his head in ap-
proval. At last, he said to himself, a religious man.
But then the man went on, "Then they nailed Him to a
cross, he died, and they put Him in a tomb. Three
days later he came out, saw His shadow, and went
back in again for six more weeks."

.ARE YOU SLEEPING, DEAR?.

THE MINISTER LIKED TO
CHIDE THE PRIEST ABOUT BIRTH CON-
TROL, SO HE THREW IN THIS LITTTLE
QUICKIE.

"THERE WAS THIS COUPLE
WHO HAD SIXTEEN CHILDREN AND SOON
MANY OF THEIR FRIENDS WERE KIDDING
THEM ABOUT TRYING BIRTH CONTROL.
ONE DAY THE FATHER GOT A LITTLE
TIRED OF ALL THIS, AND HE REBUKED HIS
FRIEND.

"IT'S GOT NOTHING IN THE
WORLD TO DO WITH BIRTH CONTROL. MY
WIFE HAS A HEARING PROBLEM, AND WE
ARE NOT GOING TO HAVE ANY MORE CHIL-
DREN. SHE'S GOTTEN HERSELF A HEAR-
ING AID. "

PERPLEXED, HE BLURTED
OUT, "WHAT'S A HEARING AID GOT TO DO
WITH IT?"

"WELL," HE MAN ANSWERED,
"BEFORE, WE USED TO GO TO BED AND I
WOULD ASK HER, " ARE WE GOING TO GO
TO SLEEP OR WHAT?"

AND SHE'D SAY, "WHAT?"

"LET ME IN, ST. PETER"

But the one I must get in here, insisted the priest, is about the Boston Writer and the young Polish Farmer who both arrived at the Pearly Gates at exactly the same time. But there was room for only one soul to enter heaven at that time.

St. Peter said, "I may have room for one more and St. Benedict has decided on a good way to determine who is most worthy to let in here. We'll pick a word, and each of you gets three minutes to write a poem with that word in it. The word, by the way, is Timbuktu. Whomever has the best poem gets in."

The guy from Boston jumped ahead of the Polish farmer, "I want to be first." For a writer, he thought to himself, this should be a piece of cake. When the three minutes were up, he recited his poem:

"Across the desert sands I stare,
My eyes all red from the sun's red glare,
But in the distance, coming into view
I see a caravan bound for Timbuktu."

"Not bad, not bad on such short notice," said St. Peter . Then he turned to the young Polish farmer and addressed him. "My friend, have you been able to write a poem for us?"

"Sure, " said the lad. "I think I've got a good one. Here it is:

A huntin' Tim and I did went,
We come upon t'ree girls in a tent
Them being t'ree and us being two,
I bucked one and Timbuktu."

- 49 -

CAN YOU PASS THE TEST?

The minister said, "I've got two quick dandies to tell you and then I've got to leave."

A missionary had come to this small town, and set up a tent in a vacant field. Next he went about the village, posting signs for services that he would conduct during the course of his stay, which was to be one month. He was pleasantly surprised when he had a rather large crowd the very first night. He was a hell and damnation preacher with a powerful message, "There simply was too much sex in the world. "

"I intend to put all the people in this town to a test. Tomorrow night, I will announce my program and its rewards." The suspense and anticipation created an even larger crowd the second night.

He started his preaching, "In order to get to heaven there is only one way, and that's to be a member of my church. In order to become a member of my church, you must pass the test. " And then he went on to explain the test. When his mission ended at the end of the month, whomever survived the test could become members of his church. The test consisted of refraining from sex for a whole month. Not surprisingly, only three couples volunteered to undergo the experiment.

At the end of the month, the first couple, both in their fifties, reported to the missionary. The man did the talking for both of them. He said, "I hope this will inspire more people, because we found it wasn't really all that difficult. For one thing we have a large house, so we can each sleep in our own bedroom. And my wife never cared all that much about it anyway. So I got used to going without sex. We did not have sex for the whole month."

"Welcome, welcome to my church. I am so happy you met the test."

The second couple responded next, and the woman gave the report. They were in their late thirties. She began, "I wouldn't say that it wasn't difficult. The first week went OK, but the second week got to me. We took a lot of cold showers, one stayed up while the other went to bed, because we sleep together, and it was mighty tough getting used to him not being there. But I am happy to report that the third week we turned to prayer and fasting, and we were able to make it through the whole month without sex."

"Welcome, welcome to my church. This is just marvelous that both of you can join my church. I say again, welcome. And what about you?" he asked as he turned to the third couple who were in their twenties.

"It was trying, very trying," said the young man. "We got by the first week, and we made it through the second week with a great deal of problems, but early in the third week, when she bent over in front of me to pick up something she had dropped on the floor, I couldn't help myself. I'm sorry, but it happened right then and there. We had sex right on the spot."

The missionary was flabbergasted and said in a heavy voice, "You know you are not welcome in my church. I'm sorry, but you are just not welcome."

"I can understand that," the young man sounded penitent, "because we're not very welcome at the Piggly Wiggly grocery right now either.!!!!"

THE BARGAIN GENIE

THE WIDOW thought it was time to inter-ject some risque humor. She wanted to liven up the party.

She told about a young fellow who was walking along the beach, day dreaming about girls. He liked girls and had known a few. He stopped to pick up a bottle, uncorked it, and a Jewish genie popped out.

The genie said, "I'm from Israel. My father was unhappy with me, so he put me in this bottle, hoping that I would gain some common sense if I rolled around in the water for a while. I floated all the way over here, and to thank you for releasing me from this bottle prison, you can have any wish you have in mind. But be careful what you wish for; I can not change it later."

There was no question in the young man's mind what he would wish for. He told the genie, "I want to be close to all the beautiful women in the world." Whereupon the genie made him a tampax.

The salty widow asked, "Do you know what the moral of the story is?" She giggled as she manipulated the crowd, "You never get anything from a Jew without a string attached to it."

HOW IS THAT AGAIN MR. GENIE?

The widow liked this kind of joke and had another one up her sleeve. Three guys were lolling on a beach, waiting for some girls to come by. Unexpectedly, a green bottle washed out of the turf and landed at their feet. They opened it, expecting to find a note, but a genie popped out. The genie said, "You can have any wish you like. But my powers of restoration only last a year. So be sure to be back here in a year, if you want to continue your life."

"OK," said the first guy. "Make me a fish, so I can swim in all the strange waters of the world."

"Abracadabra, you are now a fish. Be back in a year." And the fish swam off. The second one said, "Make me an eagle. There are a few heads I want to peck on."

"Abracadabra you are now an eagle. Don't fly too far. Be back in a year." And off he flew.

The third guy was big, brawny, and not too bright. He just said, "I want to be a stud."

"OK, if that's your wish. Be back in a year. Abacadabra you are now a stud."

A week before a year was up, the genie was waiting for them to return. The fish was the first to arrive. The genie restored him and asked how it was to be a fish. "Great," said the guy. "It was wonderful. Now restore my buddies. I'm anxious to get going."

Just then the eagle landed near them and the genie transformed him to manhood. He was elated. The two friends wanted the third buddy to come back so they could share their experiences. They waited and waited but the stud did not show up. The genie reminded them that his powers expired the next day. At the end of the next day, a tire came screaming down the beach and braked in front of them. They were shocked when they heard a voice from the tire yelling, "Get me back, get me back."

But the genie simply asked, "Where the hell have you been?"

"Stuck in a snowbank in Montana," came the reply.

I'LL BE DOGGONED

THE SALTY WIDOW interrupted, "I saw a performance by an actress and she told this beautie." An old lady was rocking back and forth in her rocking chair out on the front porch one summer evening when she noticed some kids had thrown a wine bottle on it the night before. She picked up the bottle and just for the hell of it, she pulled out the cork to see if there might be a little left. But much to her surprise, out popped a beautiful genie. The genie smiled at her and happily announced, "Thanks for letting me out. I am so happy to be free at last. For saving me, you can have three wishes. What will they be?" This old widow had straggly hair, was dressed poorly, and had no personal care. Things had not gone well for her in life. So she said, "For my first wish, I would like lots and lots of money."

"Your wish is granted," said the genie. Money fluttered down and covered the porch. "Now what is your second wish?"

She thought only a second and said, "Make me young, and beautiful, and sexy again."

"Your second wish is granted," said the genie. The woman turned into a gorgeous, young, sexy girl. "And now think carefully. What will be your last wish?"

She saw her faithful old hound dog lying next to her, and a brilliant idea came to mind. "Can you make this old hound dog of mine into a handsome prince that I can spend the rest of my days with?"

"Your last wish will be granted," said the genie, and the old hound dog was transformed into a handsome prince. She said, "Oh, I can't believe my good fortune. I'm so happy."

The handsome and charming prince looked down on her in the rocking chair and asked, "Now aren't you sorry you had me fixed?"

OUR LOVEABLE UNPREDICTABLE SENIOR CITIZENS

LOVE IN THE OLDEN DAYS

Love was simple———

　　　"Hmmmmmm............?"

　　　"AH—hmmmmm........!"

　　　"Whoa.....................!"

MORE FUN THE SECOND TIME

A peppy lady came in, sat down, listened awhile and then asked, "May I tell this true story about when I got married for the second time?" Naturally, everyone let her go on.

"On the first night of our honeymoon, we went to bed and it wasn't long before I told my new husband, "Henry {he knew my first husband} used to kiss me on the neck, and I really liked that." You see, he was a little slow, and I didn't think we had too much time to waste.

So he kissed me on the neck, and then I said, "Henry used to kiss me on my dimple, here on my chin." So he kissed my dimple and I told him I liked that."

Then I said, "Henry used to kiss me on the tip of my nose and I enjoyed that a lot." So he kissed me on the tip of my nose. Finally, I had to push him along, so I suggested, "Henry always nibbled my ear before we made love."

He got out of bed and I asked him, "What's the trouble? Where are you going?"

He answered, "I've got to get my false teeth!"

A NEW SEX CALENDAR

The salty widow wanted to be one of the boys. She could tell jokes with the best of them. She began telling about a lady who had a slight speech impediment. She had lost all her energy, and was tired all the time so she went to see her personal doctor. She told him, "I get so tired, doctor. I just have no pep at all."

"Let's find out what's wrong with you. First of all, how's your appetite? And what are you eating?"

"Oh, I eat plenty. And I have an excellent diet, too. Only the healthiest foods. And I like lots of sex."

Usually the doctor had heard plenty of women complaining about their husband's demands; this was a switch. "Hold on," he said. "Maybe that's why you are tired all the time. From now on I'd suggest that you limit your sex to days of the week that start with a [T]."

"Thay, doctor," she asked, "does that include Taturday and Tunday?"

THE MARRIAGE COUNSELOR

The priest was a great story teller. He wanted everybody to hear this one.

The marriage counselor was new to a town in Upper Michigan. He felt that he needed to introduce himself to the general populace to generate some business. So he held a party and had a rather large group in attendance. He wanted to lighten up on the subject of marriage counselling, so he began by saying, "I can usually tell how long a couple has been married, by the frequency that they indulge in sex."

When they are first married, they have sex every day and it shows. For instance, this young couple right down here in front. How long have you been married?"

The two lovebirds were holding hands, and she was almost sitting on his lap. "Three weeks," she cooed.

Then he looked around a little more and spied another couple that he felt he could approach. "I'll bet you have sex about once a week."

Looking rather glum, she answered, "Something like that."

In the back of the room, there was a guy who was at least seventy-five years old, and he was all smiles. He was strutting about like a rooster. The counselor was perplexed. He said to the old guy, "A guy of your age should be getting it about once a year. What makes you so darn happy?"

The old guy roared out loud, "Once a year is right, but tonight's the night."

"RIDE'EM COWBOY"

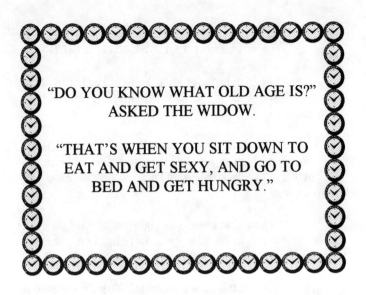

"DO YOU KNOW WHAT OLD AGE IS?"
ASKED THE WIDOW.

"THAT'S WHEN YOU SIT DOWN TO
EAT AND GET SEXY, AND GO TO
BED AND GET HUNGRY."

A CRYING SHAME

THE PRIEST continued. A man was found on the curb, crying. "What's the trouble?" asked a caring young lady. "Everything gone wrong for you?"

"No, no," said the old man. "Everything's fine. I've got a nice home, I'm retired with a good income, I married a young wife last year. She treats me great. Our sex life is wonderful."

"Well, what are you crying about then?" asked the girl.

He answered, "I can't remember where I live!!"

WON"T YOU PLEASE SIT STILL

The Irish bachelor knew he would be taking the widow home to spend the night with him after she told this raunchy tale.

A group of senior citizen tourists were on a bus, when one of them approached the driver. She told him, "There's a man back there that keeps putting his hand up my leg."

"There's an empty seat right there," said the driver, pointing to one in the front row. "Sit in that one." She no sooner sat down, and another woman came up to the driver.

She had the same complaint. "There's a man in the back of the bus who keeps putting his hand up my leg."

"Damn," said the driver, rather irritated, "I don't have enough to watch without something like that happening. Sit next to that other lady, right there."

Soon a third lady came up to the driver with the same complaint. He stopped the bus to investigate and take care of the disturbance. He walked to the back of the bus, where he found an elderly gentleman on his hands and knees between the last two rows. "What in the hell are you doing down there?" he asked.

"I'm looking for my toupee," he answered, "And I had a hold of it three times already, but it keeps getting away from me!!"

WEAK KIDNEYS

The old lady, who was a stranger in town said, "I just thought of another old timer."

An elderly couple went to the doctor for their annual exams. The husband saw the doctor first. The doctor rapped him on the knee with the hammer and he had good reflexes. The man said, "The Good Lord watches over me." The doctor went through several other routines and all came out well, each time the man reiterating, "The Good Lord watches over me." Then he told the doctor his story.

It seems he had to get up rather frequently during the night to use the bathroom. He said, "The Lord watches over me, even turning the light on and off every time I go."

When it was the wife's turn for her exam, she asked the doctor about her husband's condition. The doctor reported that her husband was in excellent health, but wondered about his story. She asked, "What did my husband tell you?" The doctor repeated the story word for word as he had heard it, and then inquired of her how the good Lord was turning the light on and off for him when he used the bathroom?

She angrily replied, "That old fool. He's been peeing in the refrigerator again!!"

MEMORIES

The old lady was not going to give up. She started again.

At the twenty-fifth wedding anniversary dance, the orchestra leader wanted to give the players a little rest, so he told the gathering, "At these dances, we have a list of favorite numbers that are most frequently requested. Newlyweds usually ask for, "More and More." Those married one year usually say, "Play Night and Day." For those married five years, we usually play, "Saturday Night." We'll play these for our first set."

After they finished, he again took the microphone and said, "Those married ten years almost always ask for, "Once in Awhile." We get less requests from those married twenty-five years, but the standard is, "Now and Then." We are going to honor our hosts with these numbers now. And then we'll play one for those married fifty years.

An old man at the dance interrupted the leader. "Now just a cotton picking minute, mister, before you play, "Memories," I wish you would play, "We Did It Before and We Can Do It Again."

THE FLYING KANGAROO

THE FLYING KANGAROO

The widow proved she was not afraid to pick on anybody as she related the tale of the two old maids who were visiting the zoo. They were fascinated by how uninhibited the animals were. These two gals liked to play practical jokes and thought this was the ideal time for one.

One said, "You know I would like to make that big kangaroo laugh. Wouldn't that be fun?"

"How in the world can you make a kangaroo laugh?" asked the other.

She said, "Just for the hell of it, I'm going to tickle him in the crotch. I'll bet he'll laugh right out loud." She reached through the bars and tickled his crotch, whereupon the kangaroo screamed, and jumped over the fence.

The zoo keeper saw the kangaroo hopping away, and ran up to the two old maids to find out what happened. The woman answered, "We were just going to make the kangaroo laugh by tickling his crotch, but he jumped out of his cage. I'm terribly sorry."

The zoo keeper dropped his trousers and said, "Here, tickle my crotch. I've got to catch that s.o.b.!!"

GET MARRIED?

ERNIE TOLD about the man who was 65 and went to see his personal physician for his annual check-up. As the doctor looked over his form, he asked, "Is your father still living?"

The man said, "Why yes, of course, and in very good health."

Then the doctor said, "We like to get a history of a man's family so we can guard against certain diseases, etc. At what age did your grandfather die?"

"Did I say my grandfather was dead? He's still going strong. In fact he's celebrating his 120th birthday by getting married. Isn't that just marvelous?"

"Now why in the world would a man of 120 want to get married?" asked the doctor.

"Did I say he wanted to get married?"

THREE STAGES IN THE LIFE OF A WOMAN

Ernie went right on telling about two girls who were sitting at the bar, looking for some male companionship, when they noticed an elderly woman had all the men in the room crowded around her. "I wonder what she has, that we haven't got?" asked one.

"She's not good looking, no figure, and just look at those guys. Like flies drawn to honey."

After a while, they engaged the older woman in conversation. One of the girls ask, "What is it that attracts all these men?"

"Well, " the older lady replied, "it's like this. When I was twenty, I gave it away, and when I was forty, I charged for it. Now that I'm in my sixties, I'm having a hell of a time buying it back!!

THE THREE STAGES OF A MAN'S LIFE

Ernie said, "There are three stages of life. The first one is when two little boys are making mud pies. They work hard at it and bring them to the front stoop of the house, calling their mothers out to look at them. 'Boy,' one of them tells his mother, 'the mud is just right, the sun is hot and they dry just right, and boy are they nice when we get done.'

"The second stage is when the two boys are now grown men, married with a start on their families, working side by side in the factory and during lunch, one says to the other, 'Boy, did my wife and I have a good time in bed last night. Things are really great.' "

"The third stage is when the two old friends are now retired, sitting in their rocking chairs on the front porch. One puts down the newspaper and says to the other, 'Boy, did I ever have a good bowel movement this morning.' "

FARMING

HIGH PRICED MANURE

The Belgian farmer was listening to Ernie long enough that he learned that these little warmer-uppers were not a bad idea so he proceeded along the same line.

He asked, "Did you hear about the dumb Belgian who spent four days in the Sears store looking for wheels for his wife's miscarriage?

The Belgian farmer had a few added tales that came to mind and he began this way:

It seems there were two farmers, Joe and Fred, who lived next to each other, had gone to court, for they couldn't resolve a conflict concerning the value of a pile of manure. A line fence separated the land of the two antagonistic farmers, but it seems Joe had gotten careless and piled manure on the line for many years. Fred didn't like this, so he removed it without Joe's permission. Joe sued Fred for a hugh sum, which of course Fred refused to pay, maintaining that manure had little or no value. In the courtroom, the judge asked Joe how he had arrived at such a high value for the pile of manure.

"Well, it's like this," he said. "I was carrying on an affair with our housekeeper, and we were having a devil of a time keeping out of my wife's sight. One day, we were making whoopee in the cornfield, and my wife came a'yelling for me. I tried to pull up my pants as fast as I could, but I didn't have time to buckle my suspenders when she met me at the end of the field."

"I know what you've been doing," she screamed at me.

"By this time the girl had run away, and I thought I could convince my wife that I had a sudden urge to go and didn't have time to get to the toilet," the man testified.

She was very jealous and she said, "We'll see about that."

The judge was getting impatient and asked, "What does all that have to do with the price of manure?"

Joe had the answer ready. "Don't you see, your honor, that right then, I would have given a million dollars for a little turd about two inches long!!"

COMMON SENSE RELIGION

The Belgian farmer thought he would finish up with this little tale. My neighbor was out plowing in the field when his fourteen year old son came running up to him, yelling, "Pa, come home quick. There's a preacher came to the house, and he's talking to mom."

He gave hurried instructions to his son, "Jimmy, run back home. Now listen, son. If it's a priest, hide the whiskey. If it's a Lutheran minister, hide the money. And if it's one of them TV evangelists, sit on mama's lap until I get there."

"DOCTOR, COME QUICK"

The Belgian farmer kept right on going.

Two Belgian farmers were treating a sick horse. One of them took a rubber hose, put it up the horse's rectum, and told his partner, "Go to his head and watch if he looks better when I blow on the hose."

After a while, he asked, "Anything happen yet?" The other fellow kept answering , "No."

Finally he said, "I can't blow anymore. Let's trade places." So the guy at the head went to the back. When he got to the back of the horse, he pulled the hose out of the horse's rectum and reversed it. The other guy yelled, "What in the hell are you doing?"

He answered, "You don't think I am going to blow on the same end of the hose you had your mouth on, do you?"

IT WASN'T THE APPLE ON THE TREE

IT WAS THE PEAR ON THE GROUND

The Belgian farmer never missed a beat, as he followed up with his tale about the wily old farmer who had been leading a double life. At every opportunity, he bedded down the pretty, young maiden, he and wife had hired to care for the children. After many years of hard work, he had an accident with the tractor. They carried him into the house, and he knew he had but a short time to live.

His wife was at his side, cradling his head in her arms. He wanted to make amends with her before he met the Lord, so he made his last confession.

"My dear wife," he began, "I haven't been as faithful to you as I should have been. Cherry, [for that was the young maiden's name], and I had quite a few rousts in the hay. But I wanted to keep a record, for I knew this day of reckoning would come, so I made a notch on the wall of the horse stall, for every time we made passionate love."

The wife went out to the barn and checked the horse stall. It was carved up something awful. There wasn't enough room for all the notches. She came back to her husband, and took him in her arms.

She said, "I'll forgive you, if you'll forgive me. Because that good looking young milk hauler and I took quite a few too. I put a bean in that jar on the cupboard every time we went to bed, and they're all there too, except the four pounds I took out for threshing!!!"

SURE IS TOUGH TO BE A FARMER

THE BELGIAN FARMER asked if they heard about the guy who took a roll of paper to a crap game?

Or about the Belgian who was so lazy he married a pregnant woman?

But the one I really wanted to tell was about the old farmer who had an accident on the farm while operating his corn picker. He had injured his arm, and although it wasn't critical it was serious. When he arrived at the hospital, there was no bed available for him, so they placed him on a gurney and set him in the hallway. Shortly after that, a young woman entered the hospital and the nurses rushed to assist her. One of them yelled, "Get her to a room."

The farmer was impatient. He asked, "What about a room for me? I was here first."

The nurses attempted to console him. "This woman is in labor!!"

"That's the way it goes all the time," he said. "Everything for labor and nothing for the poor farmer."

ROOSTER PSYCHOLOGY

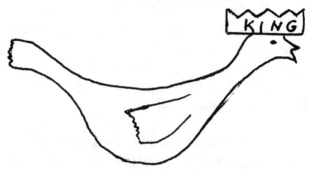

The Belgian farmer's eyes lit up again. It was his time to get in on the action. He told about the chicken farmer who had one rooster and a flock of hens. He wanted to insure fertile eggs, so he ordered another rooster from the Sears Roebuck catalog. The old rooster did not like the idea that he'd have to share some of the hens with the new upstart, so he concocted a plan to maintain his number one position.

When the new rooster arrived, the old rooster talked with him and challenged him to a race around the yard. But he insisted that because of his advanced age, he should be given a head start of approximately twenty yards.

The young rooster crowed loudly and exclaimed, "I could give you fifty yards and still beat you." The old rooster was given the choice of the day of the race.

He timed it carefully. He knew when the old farmer was about to go hunting, and would pass through the yard on his way to the woods. The race started out as planned with a twenty yard advantage for the old guy. As they came near the finish line, the old rooster slowed down, so that the younger fellow was catching up on him, which caused the farmer to raise his gun to his shoulder and shoot the young rooster.

When the farmer entered his house, he presented his wife with a dead rooster, with this explanation, "That's the third queer rooster that catalog outfit has sent me."

SO YOU LIKE ETHNIC JOKES

OFFICIAL GER- MAN FLAG	OFFICIAL POL- ISH FLAG
Blue	White
Red	
Yellow	Red

UNOFFICIAL GERMAN FLAG	UNOFFICIAL POLISH FLAG

OFFICIAL FRENCH
FLAG

OFFICIAL FLAG OF
BELGIUM

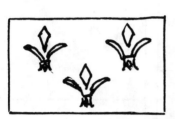
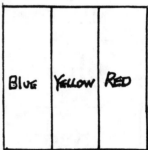

UNOFFICIAL FRENCH
FLAG

UNOFFICIAL FLAG OF
BELGIUM

THE EVER LOVING POLISH

WOW!
I WON THE $1 MILLION
DOLLAR POLISH
LOTTERY!!!

But in the POLISH LOTTERY
you get a dollar a year for a
million years.

OH, YOU BEAUTIFUL FROG

Ernie liked to tell Polish jokes. It seems everybody likes to tell Polish jokes. Especially the Polish people. When this Polish mother's teenage daughter failed to respond to several raps on the door when her mother attempted to arouse her in the morning, the mother entered the room. She was shocked, for sleeping next to the pretty young daughter was a handsome young man.

When the girl finally awoke, she said, "Mother. You don't understand. I was walking next to the stream out back, and a frog came up to me and said if I kissed him, he would turn into a handsome prince, and here he is."

Ernie asked, "Would you believe a story like that?" He was pulling the crowd's leg. "Her mother didn't either."

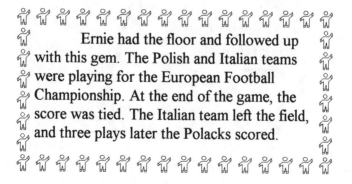

Ernie had the floor and followed up with this gem. The Polish and Italian teams were playing for the European Football Championship. At the end of the game, the score was tied. The Italian team left the field, and three plays later the Polacks scored.

A POLISH ROCKET SCIENTIST???

The Belgian farmer thought he would be home free telling this joke about an Englishman, a Frenchman, and a Polack. They were three rocket scientists who were selected to take a year long trip to Mars. This was a highly sought after and coveted excursion. They were told they could each bring the one thing most important to them, but the weight limit was 100 pounds.

The Englishman said he could not go a whole year without English chocolate, so he took a hundred pounds. The Frenchman siad he could not get along without a girl for that long a period, so he brought a little girl of less than 100 pounds. The Polack brought 100 pounds of Cuban cigars.

When they returned from the year long flight, the Englishman is the first off the rocket, and it is plain to see that he ate all the chocolates for he has gained considerable weight. The Frenchman gets off next with his little girl and she now has a baby. The Polack comes down the ramp, carrying his 100 pounds of cigars, with one in his mouth. The first thing he asks, "Anybody got a match?"

THE TRUCK DRIVER

A Polish lad was taking an exam to qualify for an available truck driving job . He was able to answer all the questions until he came to one which asked, "If you are driving down a mountain road and your brakes failed, your partner is sleeping in the cab behind you, there's a shear wall on your left, and a steep drop-off on your right, what would you do?"

He wrote, "I would wake up Leroy. He ain't never seen no serious accident before."

"ALLIGATOR-YOU'RE OUT"

The Belgian farmer related how he had stopped for lunch in Pulaski and overheard two guys telling this joke. Two local young men were sitting in a tavern in Pulaski, trying to determine how they could make some big money, quicklike.

One said, "I understand that alligator shoes are bringing a hell of a big price these days. Maybe we can cash in on that."

The second one said, "Let's head for Florida. They've got a lot of alligators there."

"Sounds good," said the first one. "We'll need some ropes," and they soon were on their way to Florida.

When they arrived, they drove to the water's edge, took one look at the big ugly creatures, and decided they needed some fortification before they embarked on their endeavor.

After quite a few beers, one of them jumped in the water, and began to wrestle the alligator. After a fierce struggle, he finally subdued the beast, turned it over on its back, and yelled to his friend, "We're going to have to try another. This one ain't got no shoes on!!"

OUCH!!!

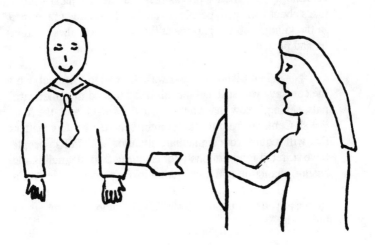

      Ernie asked, "Did you ever hear of Polish Cuff Links?"
      "No, what about them?"
      "They pierce their wrists!!"

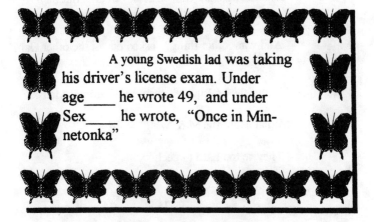

      A young Swedish lad was taking his driver's license exam. Under age____ he wrote 49, and under Sex____ he wrote, "Once in Minnetonka"

"STOP, I SAY, STOP"

Almost everybody is Catholic in this little Polish community, but good sports as they are, they frequently tell jokes about their own people. Ernie had heard one of the men in the village, tell the patrons at the coffee shop, these funnies he had picked up.

When Bishop Medski was elevated to Cardinal, while the conclave was still assembled, he addressed the other cardinals, saying, "Now that I am Cardinal Medski, and the first Polish Cardinal from this community, there are a few matters that will require your immediate attention. The Polish people have suffered ignominiously for centuries with degrading, debasing, shameful, and humiliating jokes. Now that I am a Cardinal, and can do something about it, I want to use every resource at your command, to stop all Polish joke telling around the world."

"Oh, I can't foresee a problem with that at all." answered one of the Cardinals. "Now that you are a Cardinal to our credit from this district, we will contact every newspaper, radio station, television station, comedian, and ask them to refrain from telling any more Polish jokes. We will take care of this immediately, your Highness."

Cardinal Medski said, "Thank you all. And then there's this other thing, I wish you would take care of also."

"And what other thing?" asked one of the other Cardinals.

"About the M & M's," answered Cardinal Medski.

"What about the M & M's?"

"They're too hard to peel."

DO I GET THE JOB?

A young man was taking a test for a job being offered. On the application was a question which asked, "Old McDonald had a _____. How do you spell the answer to this question?"

He wrote <u>e-i-e-i-o</u>.

ERNIE went on to say that you could always tell when it was spring time in Pulaski, because all the syrup pails were hanging on the telephone poles.

Ernie's funny bone was tickling. He couldn't resist mentioning that Bell Telephone wanted to install a new system in the village, but they stopped when one of the board members said, "We already have TACO BELL."

DID YOU HEAR ABOUT THE BELGIAN LESBIAN?

"SHE LIKED BOYS!!!"

GREEN SIDE UP

The pharmacist said he had just heard this one from a local developer. All that was left for the contractor to complete the house, was for the new owner to select paint colors for the interior. He made an appointment with the lady purchaser. He said, "The best way to do this, is for us to go from room to room, discuss it, and then I will write the color you selected on the wall. That way it is impossible to make a mistake."

They started in one of the bedrooms. She selected a color, he wrote it on the wall, opened a window and yelled, "Green side up."

He repeated the same thing as they went from room to room, and finally the suspense was too great for her. She asked, "What in the world is this 'Green Side Up' that you keep yelling out the window ?"

"Oh, I've got a bunch of Swedes laying sod today."

THE POLISH DETECTIVE

"Three men were being interviewed for a policeman's job," the priest began. "All the candidates had similar qualifications which made it difficult for the police chief to decide who to hire. He said, "I will ask one last question of each of you to help me make a decision."

He asked the Jewish lad who had applied, "Who killed Jesus Christ?" The Jewish boy replied, "The Romans."

Next he asked an Italian lad the same question, and he answered, "The Jews." Then he asked the Polish man the same question. "Let me think about that a little. Can I get back to you next week with my answer?"

The Chief thought it unusual, but said, "I guess I can wait." The Polish man went home, and his wife asked, "Did you get the job?"

"Oh sure," he said. "It was a piece of cake. I not only got the job, but they've already got me working on a murder case."

THE IRISH SCHOOL TEACHER

The Irish bachelor was somewhat shy, but liked to laugh at his own group. He told about the Irishman who had taken a wrong turn and stopped at a tavern to get directions He found two Polish men at the bar.

"Before I give you directions," laughed one of them, "I'd like to tell about the Polish man who was having difficulty remembering, etc. He decided to get a physical and it was determined he needed brain surgery. While he was having the surgery, the doctors had his head open in order to make a thorough evaluation."

The head surgeon said, "This is worse than I imagined. His brain will have to be removed if we wish to save his body." So they removed his brain and started sewing him up. They were finished and about to wheel him back to his room, when suddenly he jumped up, and ran out of the hospital. "You know where they finally caught up to him, five years later?"

"No, where?"

"Teaching school in Ireland!

THE BLARNEY STONE

The Irishman didn't want to lose his turn, so he continued with this article about the Blarney Stone that also was featured in the Irish Free Press:
The Irish for years have revered it to the extent of kissing it often for good luck. However, it has recently been found that the Blarney Stone, is in reality, the petrified ass of a Polack.

PREPARING THE IRISH SERMON

The Irish bachelor went on to tell about a well travelled and notorious Irishman who had died, and the parson had the job of preparing a good sermon for the funeral. The old Irish priest knew the fellow well; he drank, caroused, cheated on his wife, was a poor worker, and in general there was very little he could possibly think of to use in his sermon. But since it was the custom he have something good to say about every person resting in the coffin on the day of his funeral, the priest went to see the man's wife.

"You've lived with this man for forty years. Surely you'll help me prepare a proper sermon for him. I need your help, my good woman. Was he a good provider?"

"No, that he wasn't atall," she answered, "I had to beg for food most of the time."

"Was he a good father?" the priest was searching for a good point.

"No, he beat the kids every time they got in his way."

Although the priest knew the answer to this one, he asked, "Wasn't he a good and faithful man?"

"No, not atall," she replied. "He took every woman to bed that he got a chance."

"Did he belong to any organizations? " asked the good Father.

She had a meager education, and asked, "What does that mean?"

"You know," he said. "Like the Klu Klux Klan."

"What are they?" she asked.

"Oh," he had to think about an explanation, and then he studdered and stammered and said, "You know, they're like devils under a sheet."

She got big eyes and answered excitedly, "Oh, that he was, Father. A devil under the sheets. That he was, Father!!!!"

- 86 -

THE KENNEDY FAMILY

The Irishman laughed loudly as he started telling about the following article that appeared in the Irish Free Press:

At the time of the events at Chappaquiddick, the Irish government was faced with something of a dilemma, since the Irish people have such great reverence for the Kennedy family.

After much consideration, the government decided to comment via diplomatic cable to the United States, which was simultaneously made public to the Irish people. The cable read as follows:

God bless Senator Kennedy, that sainted soul who was taking that fine Catholic girl to midnight mass when the tragedy occurred. Noble man that he was, he remained at the scene of the accident for nine hours in devout prayer. The American government would be well advised to find the Protestant bastards who built that bridge.

NEVER TELL A LIE

A car full of celebrating , young, Irishmen were headed home from the pub one evening, and missed a turn in the road. Their car careened down a steep incline, and burst into fire. When the rescue vehicles arrived, it appeared to be too late for the victims, so they buried the entire wreckage.

"Couldn't do anything for them, eh?' asked the coroner.

"Well, there was a couple that said they were still alive, but you know how them Irishmen lie."

When a chef using his skill mixes many different herbs, vegetables, and fragrances together, what do you get?

A delicious meal.

And when an artist using his unique ability, mixes many different paint colors together, what do you get?

A beautiful picture.

And when you mix an assortment of jokes together that do not fit into any particular category, what do you get? A great addition to the best collection of jokes in the world!!! That's why we called this section - -

POT - POURRI

THE JOKE'S ON ME

Billy Bugger didn't have very many to tell, but when he did tell one, it was a dandy. Just like this one-of-a-kind. A young man committed a felony and landed in jail. The jail was very crowded so he had to share a cell with a much older prisoner. Shortly after arriving at the institution, all the prisoners were out in the main yard for their daily exercise. During a rest period, one of the men yelled, "44." Everyone burst out laughing. Then someone yelled, "36." Uncontrolled laughter again. Again an inmate called out, "28." Uproarious laughter.They returned to their cells, and the young felon asked his older cellmate, "What gives out there? A guy yells out a number and everybody laughs."

"This is the way it is," the old fellow answered. "We've all been confined here for so long, that we know every joke by heart. There aren't any new ones, so we don't bother wasting the time to tell the joke; we simply call out the number of the joke instead. Everybody has the numbers memorized and they know what joke it stands for."

"Where do you get the numbers?" asked the young fellow.

"Here is a pamphlet the library prints, that has all the jokes and their numbers," he said as he handed him the little book. So the young man studied the booklet thoroughly, memorizing every joke so he could appreciate the jokes when they were called out in the courtyard. After he became more familiar with the other inmates, he thought he would call out a number of one that particularly tickled his funny bone.

At the first opportunity, he yelled out, "32."

Dead silence. So he thought maybe that's one I liked, but it's not necessarily the funniest joke in the book. I'll try another, so he called out, "29."

Nothing happened. Nobody laughed. So he said to himself, "I'll try one more time. "51."

No response. When they got back to their cell, he asked his partner, "When the other guys call out numbers, everybody laughs, and when I do, nobody even cracks a smile. What goes on? Don't they like me?"

"Nah," said the old guy, "it's nothing like that. Some fellows can tell a joke, and others can't!!!"

THE EAGLE WHO LOST ITS MATE

Ernie wanted to get one more in before everyone retired for the evening. He told about the eagle who had lost its mate. Eagles are monogamous and this particular one was especially lonesome after his mate disappeared. He desperately needed some female loving and companionship. He circled around and could not find a female eagle, so he comandeered the first flying creature he came to, and forced it down to his nest.

Apparently, this little creature, a dove, was afraid of such a large bird, so she cried, "I'm a dove, but I don't make love. "

"Well then, out with you," he said. This experience only fired up his desire more than before. He took off again, and spied another bird. He wasn't very particular, as he forced a loon to settle in his nest.

She squeaked in a high pitched squirrely tune, "I'm a loon, and I want to spoon." She sounded absolutely eerie. "Now I know where the expression "looney bird" comes from," he said. Much as he wanted a female, this bird really turned him off. He kicked her out of the nest, and made another quest for a desirable female. Soon he found another bird, and forced it to land in his nest.

"Finally, I'm in luck," he squawked to himself. "I've got myself a duck. Now if she'll only sing me a tune like the loon, everything will be ducky."

But the duck yelled, "I'm a drake; you made a mistake."

-90-

EMMALINA BROWN

The _____ church [insert your own
name] were holding their women's auxiliary meeting to
nominate their slate of candidates to act as officers of their
church for the following year. When the president asked for
nominations from the floor, a lady stood up and said, "I
nominate Emmalina Brown."

Immediately, another woman jumped up and said,
"Emmalina Brown? You nominate Emmalina Brown? She
ain't got no class!"

Stunned by the accusation, there was a moment of
silence. Then a rather large woman in the back of the room
did not agree. She held her ground. She said, " I'm Emmalina Brown. And you say I ain't got no class? Who do you
think influenced the pastor to install the pink and yellow
stained glass windows in this church? Ah did! And who do
you think had the school house painted that beautiful
chartreuse color? Ah did. And who do you think donated
that fuchsia tapestry behind the baptismal font? Ah did.
And you say I ain't got no class! Sh-i-i-it!!!"

I THINK I MARRIED A NUN

When the daughter and her new husband came
back from their honeymoon, they went to the home of her
parents. The father retired to the living room with his new
son-in-law and asked him, "How does it feel to be a member of this family? I hope you are very happy!"

The young man answered, "I would have been
happy, but I think I married a nun. None in the morning,
none at noon, and none at night!"

"Come out in the kitchen and meet Mother Supe-
rior," said the father.

WHAT A CHISELER!!!

The widow wanted to do this gem.

"It seems there was a young man from Montreal who was attending a convention in Toronto. He was very interested in the French couple in the next room. He had seen them holding hands in the restaurant and was pleasantly surprised when they entered the room next to his. He knew they would be making love and he wanted to listen in on them. He had never indulged himself, so this was a big thing for him. He had heard that if you took a water glass and pressed it to the wall, it would magnify the sound considerably. So he did this, and found he could hear every word .

The Frenchman started by telling his young paramour, "I love that dimple you have in your chin. I've got a friend in Montreal who I would like to have chisel that in granite."

She answered, "Oh, I just love it when you trace your finger over it so slowly."

Next, he said, "You have the finest features, especially your nice slim neck. I wish I could get my friend in Montreal to chisel it in granite to keep it the same forever."

She said, "Keep rubbing my neck. That feels so good."

The young man from Montreal was getting very excited. The Frenchman was moving right along. He was telling her, "You've got the most beautiful, firm, well rounded breasts I have ever seen."

The young man couldn't contain himself any longer. He pulled back from the wall, the glass dropped and smashed into a thousand pieces. It made so much noise that the Frenchman came to the separating door as he knew someone was listening to him. He yelled, "What in the hell are you doing in there? And who the hell are you?"

"I'm the chiseler from Montreal," he replied. "And I'm ready to start chiseling."

GOVERNMENT IS TOPS

Ernie said, "I've got one more that I picked up at that Quebec convention. Four Quebec men met in the coffee shop and were discussing how smart each of their dogs were. The first one was from IBM. The man carried a little blackboard and said his dog could match calculations and was named T-Square. He instructed the dog to go to the blackboard and draw a circle, a square, and a triangle, which the dog did easily.

The next guy was from Westinghouse and said his dog was even smarter. The dog's name was Slide Rule and was told to fetch a dozen cookies and divide them into four piles of three. The dog accomplished this task with ease.

The third dog owner, who came from GE said that was good, but his dog was even better. His dog's name was Measure. The owner told him to get a quart of milk and pour seven ounces into a ten ounce glass. The dog did so. All agreed that these dogs were very smart indeed.

Then they turned to the government worker and asked, "What can your dog do?"

The government worker called his dog, who was named Coffee Break, and said to him, "Now show what you can do."

Coffee Break ate the cookies, drank the milk, screwed the other three dogs, claimed he had injured his back, filed for Workman's Compensation, and left for home on sick leave.

GIVE IT A TRY OLD CHAP

A young chap who was travelling through the area, stopped for a soda, listened a while, and then with his English accent also participated. He related how he knew of Old England and that these stories actually happened.

A fellow was riding through the English countryside when he heard a cry for help. Soon he came upon an unfortunate fellow who was up to his neck in quicksand.

"I say, there, old chap. Throw me a line if you will, please."

"Why sure, can you tuck it under your arms, man, and I'll give you a tug."

They tried, but it was useless. "Sorry, old man," said the rider, "but I don't think we're going to get you out."

He was about to coil his rope and take off when the stuck man called out, "Wait. Let's give it one more try. This time I'll take my feet out of the stirrups."

PROTECT HER HONOR

The young Englishman had still another tale to tell. Everyone there had heard of the Knights of the Round Table at one time or another, so he was on safe ground. The king had ordered this young knight to put down a disturbance in one of his provinces. The young knight summoned his squire and gave him instructions of things to do while he was away. Finally he came to a very sensitive subject; guarding his pretty wife. "I've had her fitted with a chastity belt, and I would like for you to look after her," were his parting words.

The mighty gate was lowered, the horses thundered out of the castle, and they were on their way. They had gone only a short distance when they caught sight of a young rider pushing his horse to the limit to catch up with them. They stopped, and in a few minuites, the knight saw that it was his young squire.

"What has gone wrong?" asked the knight.

"You forgot to give me the key," answered the young squire.

THE LADY AND HER DOG

After everyone gave him a good sized ovation, he continued to talk about his beloved birthplace.England is a left handed country; they drive on the left side of the road and eat with their fork in their left hand. Perhaps this is what inspired the following episode: A lady and her dog got on the bus. The driver warned her that if the dog made any noise or interfered with the comfort of any of the passengers, he would have to put the dog off the bus. She agreed to his terms. What the driver didn't count on, was that the woman was far more obnoxious than the dog. She complained about the driver's speed, his conversation with another passenger, the heat, the light, and the braking. Finally even the dog started to yelp.

The driver took this as a good omen; he would get rid of the dog, and she would surely follow. So he stopped and unloaded the dog. But the lady persisted in continuing her ride.

As soon as the bus started moving , the complaining began anew.. One of the friendly passengers, seated close to the driver, said , "I think you got rid of the wrong bitch!!"

I AM A MEMBER OF THE ROYAL GUARD

This young Englishman was having the time of his life, so he went right on. It's a great and well recognized honor to be a member of the Royal Guard at Buckingham Palace. One of the qualificatons is that a member never flinches while he is on guard. No matter what happens, he must look straight ahead, and even if he were stung by a bee, he must maintain his posture and poise, showing no discomfort or pain.

This one member was being tried in the court for his fitness to remain in this prestigious service, for he had flinched on the job. At his trial, he was given the opportunity to explain the situation, for he had an enviable record, and they did not want to dismiss him.

"It was like this, your Honor. I was standing guard, and out of the corner of me eye, across the yard, I spied a little squirrel playing on the lawn. But mind you, your Honor, I looked straight ahead and did not flinch. Soon after, out of the corner of me eye, but looking straight ahead, I did not flinch, your Honor, I saw that there was another little fellow came to join him. They played, and kept coming closer to me all the time. They bounded over the road, and came right up to me, but I did not flinch, your Honor.

"One of the little buggers ran right up the inside of my pant leg, but I did not flinch, your Honor. Then the other little bugger ran up the inside of the other pant leg, but I did not flinch, your Honor. Now there was one on each side, and they nestled in right next to my testicles, your Honor, but I did not flinch.

"But when I heard one of them say to the other, "Should we eat them now, or bury them in the park, I flinched.."

HARK I HEAR THE CANNON ROAR

Ernie pulled a piece of paper out of his pocket and said, "I've carried this around for years. It's one of my favorites." A young Englishman wanted to pursue an acting career, so he applied for a part in a play that was being put on at the local theatre. Since he had no experience, they assigned him a minimal part in this Shakespearean skit. He would have a one line role; but the director told him, "You never can tell what will happen if you perform this well. You could really impress the audience and it might propel you onto the stage in much bigger parts. But first, you must study to get this line right." He handed him the script and said, "Go home and practice until you can say it without even thinking."

Near the end of the play, his line was, "Hark, I hear the cannon roar." So the young man practiced and practiced. He walked around for days experimenting by putting more emphasis on different syllables. People would meet him on the street and thought he had gone berserk, for all he said was, "Hark, I hear the cannon roar." Finally, he had settled on the way he thought it sounded best. He was ready for rehearsal. During the rehearsal, the director told him, "Right here we'll have a simulated cannon, and you will say your line."

He said, "Hark I hear the cannon roar."

"Very good," said the director. "You did fine. I think we are ready for the big night."

He went home, grinning all the way. He would be an actor at last. He repeated the line over and over so he would be ready when his big moment arrived.

The next night, he joined the other actors on stage, and when it came to his part, an aide blasted off a blank in a shotgun, which was supposed to be the cannon roaring. The would-be actor turned around excitedly, and yelled, "Who in the hell shot that dammed gun off?"

OH MY PRINCE, PLEASE SAVE ME

The young Englishman definitely had a good sense of humor, and was greatly appreciated by the crowd. He began by telling them about this young school girl who was doing her home work. As an incentive to develop her vocabulary, the teacher had assigned her the task of composing a story without using the same verb twice. The teacher intended that she would use the dictionary, but the little girl cheated when she came to the word "save" and went directly to her father for help.

"What is another word that means the same as "save"? she asked.

Her father was reading the evening paper and had a hard time focusing on the question. He fumbled around and said, "Well, you would be conservative, or miserly, or a better word would be frugal."

"Thanks, Dad," she answered as she went back to composing her tale.

The next day, she delivered her composition to the class. This is what she said:

A prince was riding through the forest looking for somebody to save, because that's what princes are supposed to do. He came upon an animal trap, which was really a big hole in the ground, and a girl who had fallen in, was yelling for help. He jumped down the hole, frugalled her, and they lived happily ever after.

I KNOW HOW TO COUNT

The Belgian farmer told about the man who was accumulating a large family. Each time another child was born, his wife yelled, "That's enough." But the children kept coming. The father vowed that if they ever got to twelve, he would do away with himself.

They got to twelve. He went out in the woodshed, stepped on a box, tied a rope to a rafter, and made a noose which he put around his neck. He reflected for a while, and reflected some more, and finally he removed the noose. He stepped off the box and said, "I think I'm hanging the wrong man."

MEMORY LAPSE

The elderly lady, who had joined the storytellers said, "Hold on a minute, I've got one to tell here."

Three elderly women, who lived together were gathered in the living room. One said, "I am going upstairs to take a shower." She got half way up the stairway, turned to her partners and said, "I can' t remember if I took a shower or not."

The second woman chastised her. "I'll go up and see if the towels are wet, and then we'll know if you took a shower or not." When she got half way up the stairs, she looked at her partners, and in a daze asked, "Was I going upstairs or downstairs?"

The third woman said, "Boy, I'm glad I'm not as bad off as you two. You can't remember anything. I"m so happy, I'll knock on wood. Is there somebody at the front door or the back door?"

LET'S GO ON A SAFARI

The Belgian farmer continued by telling about going on a safari, and in their travels, one noon they ended up in a cannibal restaurant. They checked the menu board and discovered the following listings for dinner:

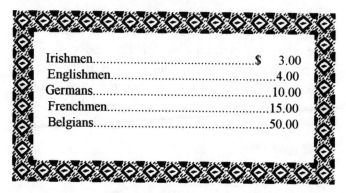

```
Irishmen..............................$    3.00
Englishmen.................................4.00
Germans..................................10.00
Frenchmen................................15.00
Belgians.................................50.00
```

The natural question of the waiter was, "How come Belgians cost so much?"

The waiter replied, "Did you ever try to skin one of those bastards?"

Ernie had a few quickies to throw in.

DO UNTO OTHERS AND THEN BEAT IT!

HOT PANTS USED TO BE A CONDITION;
NOW IT'S CHANGED INTO A FASHION.

LOVE THY NEIGHBOR,
BUT DON'T GET CAUGHT.

TAKE YOUR PICK

The pharmacist liked kids, so he thought of this one. The teacher asked the three children to each write a short story on the subject "If You Had Your Choice, What Would You Like To Be?"

The first boy wrote, "I'm a fisherman so I would like to be a fish. Boy, would I have fun., frustrating all the fishermen. I'd nibble on their hooks, get them all excited, and never take the bait. Another thing, I could swim around and look up and see everybody and everything in the water. I think being a fish would be wonderful."

The second boy wrote, "I would like to be a bird. Fly around, up and down, look over everything that's going on. I could be above it all, not having to be on the ground at all if I didn't want to. Another thing, I could look back, find all the people who treated me badly, and crap on their heads. That would give me the greatest satisfaction in the whole world."

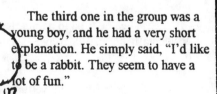

The third one in the group was a young boy, and he had a very short explanation. He simply said, "I'd like to be a rabbit. They seem to have a lot of fun."

FOR THE LOVE OF PETE

The gist of this little gag was directly opposite from the type of character the know-it-all was, but he liked to tell it anyway. He said this flour miller had an only child; a very homely daughter, and he was trying hard to get the hired man to marry her. She was also a very simple girl. The hired man talked it over with his friend, telling him that the father had promised he could have the mill, build a house, and that he would get all his money when the father died. If he married the daughter. But the prospect of making love to her, was revolting to him. His friend said, "For that kind of money, you can always throw a bag over her head."

He finally consented to marry her, and every time he made love to her, he would say "for the love of Pete". Pete was her father and he did it only for the money.

After they moved into their new house, they were hanging pictures, and he asked her to get a hammer. Being an obedient soul, she responded, "Get the hammer, get the hammer, get the hammer."

When she returned, he asked why she had not brought a nail. She said, "Get the nail, get the nail, get the nail."

When he tried to pound the nail into the wall, he accidentally hit his finger and exclaimed, "Oh, for the love of Pete!"

She started to run, yelling,"Get the bag, get the bag, get the bag..."

THE BEAR IS STRONGER
but
THE RAM IS SMARTER

The young Englishman said, "I really admire this group. They really enjoy a good joke; just for the sake of the fact that a good joke is fun, no matter what the subject matter. That's more the way, life should be." Then he told about the little Jewish boy who was seated between two large Arab men while taking a plane trip. One of the big Arab men felt he could take advantage of the young Jewish boy, so he said, "Jew boy, get me a beer."

When the little Jewish boy returned to his seat, he found that the big Arab man had crapped in his shoe. It wasn't long before the other Arab gave the little boy the same order, "Jew boy, get me a beer."

Again when the Jewish boy returned, he found the Arab had crapped in his other shoe.

The Arab drank his beer and ordered a second bottle. When he finished this one, he looked at the little guy and said, "I guess us Arabs will never get along with you Jews."

The little Jew boy responded, "Not as long as you poopoo in my shoes and I peepee in your beer."

MOTIVATE YOUR CHILDREN

THE GERMAN SEED SALESMAN
wanted to tell about the German industrialist who
had a family of six children. He called them all together for a big banquet as he had an important announcement.

This was the reason for the banquet. He began, "I am thankful for my beautiful family. You all
have wonderful wives, and I am thankful for that
also. But I have not realized one of my fondest
dreams; I do not have grandchildren. So, as an incentive, I am right now, here on the spot, offering
$50,000 to which ever one of you produces the first
grandchild. Now let us bow our heads and offer our
prayers for this wonderful meal..

Since he sat at the head of the table, he offered the prayers. "Thank you Lord for all the bless-
ings You have bestowed on our family, especially
for the fine food of which we about to partake, and
the beautiful grandchildren that I anticipate will be
joining us soon after the incentive I just made."

When he was through praying, he said,
"Now let us eat." But when he looked up, he was
the only one at the table.

YOU TELL ME YOUR DREAMS, AND I'LL TELL YOU MINE

Ernie always had a few warmer-uppers to get everybody in the mood for his "big one".

A man went to the doctor because he was tired all the time. The doctor questioned him about his activities, finally suggesting that he should cut out half his sex life.

The man asked,"Which half, doctor? The talking or the thinking part?"

Ernie was certainly not the most dedicated employee the canning company ever had, but he was one of the most lovable because he had an unending supply of good jokes. Ernie happened to be proud of his bald head; he called it a solar panel for a sex machine. So he demonstrated for the group as he told this tale about a bald headed man.

A fellow wanted to tease his friend who was bald, so as he walked by him, he ran his hand ever so slowly over the fellow's bald head and quipped, "Why that's so tender and smooth. It feels just like my wife's fanny!"

The bald fellow ran his hand over his bald head just as his friend had done and remarked, "Dammed if it doesn't."

X MARKS THE SPOT

The Belgian farmer told about the two Frenchmen who went fishing for perch in Lake Ontario. Soon they were catching one after the other. "Boy, this is great," said one. "We really should mark this spot."

"Good idea," said the other as he found a pencil in his jacket pocket and proceeded to put an X on the side of the boat.

"What are you doing that for?"

"You told me to mark this spot. And I did."

"You dummy. Next time we might get a different boat!!"

"THAT HURTS"

"But how about this one?" Ernie went on.
Three conventioneers were out on the town. One of them
had too much to drink, so his partners decided that walking
back to their hotel might tend to sober him up. On the way,
they passed a building from which they heard loud music
and a lot of noise. As they passed one of the windows, a man
came flying through and landed on the sidewalk in front of
the three men.

"What in hell is going on in there?" asked the
drunk.

"They're holding an Elk's Ball," came the reply.

"Well, tell them to let go of it, before he kicks the
dammed wall down!!"

I DON"T BELIEVE IT

A state trooper had pulled a man off the road and
was about to ticket him for speeding, when the speeder
put the pedal to the floor and took off. Again the trooper
followed and eventually was successful in pulling him
over again. This time he took no chances, pulling his gun
and ordering the man out of the car.

The trooper angrily said, "I've heard every story in
the book about all the reasons fellows have for what you just
did. But you better have the best story yet."

The man looked over the policeman very carefully.
Finally he offered this reason. "My wife ran off with a state
trooper this morning. He looked just like you. And the way
you were chasing me, I thought you were trying to bring
her back."

SERGEANT PRESTON'S LAW OF THE WILD

Ernie cmmented how fortunate he was to have a job that did not tie him down to any specific location. He said he felt much like Sergeant Preston's team of huskies.

THE SCENERY ONLY CHANGES FOR THE LEAD DOG

"HOW MUCH AM I OFFERED???"

Ernie wanted his turn again. "Everyone will believe you more if you tell them Ben Franklin said it," said Ben Franklin. And everyone will appreciate a joke more, if you tell them it's one of the great comedian's favorite.

A city dweller had a pet fenced off in the front yard, which annoyed his neighbor terribly. For you see this was a ritzy neighborhood and the pet was a pig. But the neighbor was also a friend, so he wanted to maintain a good relationship with him, at the same time plotting how he could get rid of the pig. He hinted and hawed about how the area would be improved if he had a lawn like everybody else, which, of course, would necessitate getting rid of the pig. But the neighbor always countered, "I couldn't possibly eat him, I won't sell him or give him away either. I love him."

One day the neighbor thought he had a great idea. He suggested to the man that the pig would be very happy if he took him to the zoo. "Great idea," said the pig's owner. The next morning, the neighbor was greatly relieved when he saw the man take the cushion out of the back seat of the car, and load the pig. "Gone at last," he said to himself.

He was greatly dismayed, when about three in the afternoon, he saw the car come down the street with the pig looking out the window.

"What happened?" he quickly asked the owner as he let the pig out in the front yard.

"That was an absolutely great idea you had there, taking him to the zoo. He enjoyed it so much, that tomorrow, I'm taking him to Disneyland."

HOOKED

THE MAIL carrier came in and the butcher said, "Every time I see you, I think of the three biggest lies in the world."

"Why are you reminded of that?" asked the widow.

"You will understand after I tell you the lies:

1. The check is in the mail,
2. I'll respect you just as much in the morning, and
3. I'm from the government and I'm here to help you!!"

IT'S LATER THAN YOU THINK

While the widow had their attention, she quickly got this one off, as it tickled her funny-bone.

Two sisters lived together and were afraid of males. They had little contact with men and even kept their female cat indoors at all times in fear that she might come in contact with a tomcat. The only time they talked to men was at their church. One of the girls met a nice man, dated, and eventually they were married.

They left on their honeymoon, and after being gone for a week, the homebound sister heard from the bride. She received a very short message on a postal card. It read; "Let the cat out."

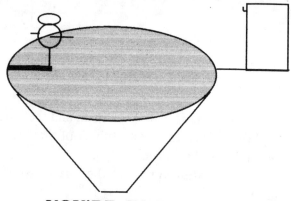

YOU'RE IN TEXAS

The pharmacist told the others to hold up; he wanted his turn. When the crowd quieted down, he said there was this fellow who was consumed with his passion to set foot in every one of the continental forty eight states. This would fulfill his life long desire. He had already made forty seven and was passing over the boundary into Texas, the last state he needed to accomplish his goal.

It was a hot, dry, summer day as he crossed over the border from New Mexico. He was dying for something to drink, but he drove quite a ways before reaching a bar. He quickly ordered a martini.

The bartender presented him with the biggest martini he had ever seen. "Boy," he exclaimed, "you call that a martini. That's more like a fish bowl."

The bartender had a ready answer. "Remember, you're in Texas. We do everything BIG here."

The guy sipped on this giant martini, and then asked the bartender for a few hors d'oeuvres as he was hungry as well as thirsty. The bartender went back to the kitchen and reappeared carrying a large plate, bearing a fillet mignon, which he promptly set down before the traveller.

"Crimonee," he exclaimed. "I asked for a few hor d'oeuvres and you plop down this big fillet mignon."

"Remember. You're in Texas. We do everything BIG here."

So the guy ate the fillet and finished the martini. By this time he needed to make a trip to the bathroom, and asked the bartender for directions, as it was a very BIG place. The bartender accommodated him, he slipped off the bar stool and started down the long hallway to the bathroom. He wasn't used to drinking martinis from a fishbowl, was a little woozy, so he braced himself as he staggered down the hall. He also forgot the instructions he had received, and when he came to the end of the hall, he turned left, instead of right, and fell into the swimming pool.

He thrashed around, and finally came up for air, yelling, **"Don't flush it!!!!**

FIREPOWER

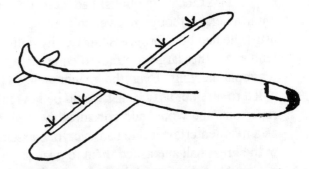

The butcher said, "Almost anything is possible with the right motivation."

Two geese were flying over the Baltimore airport at the same time that a four engine jet was taking off. They collided, the geese fell to the ground, completely oblivious as to what had transpired. Slowly, they regained consciousness.

One said to the other as they watched the big plane flying overhead, "Look at that big bird fly."

The other replied, "If you had four rear ends, and they were all on fire, you'd fly too."

LISTEN CAREFULLY

Then the Belgian farmer went on to say that the best advice he ever got, was from a realtor. When we were newly married, and looking for a house, he said,

"GET A LOT WHILE YOU'RE YOUNG."

WATCH ME MOM

A YOUNG hypnotist had wanted to be an entertainer. Although not yet an accomplished artist, he had been progressing steadily until he had landed a rather large contract to entertain at a professional meeting. Everything went well, so he decided to attempt a trick that would be new in his repertoire and would add considerably to his value as a mass entertainer. He had everyone assembled in the great hall and asked them to gaze at his hand.

He held a watch by a chain and swung it gently, back and forth, back and forth, saying the same words over and over, "You are under my command, you are under my command." After a minute or two, he felt he had everyone's undivided attention. He was exuberant; the spell was working. They were all hypnotized; the first time he had tried mass hypnotism. Now was the time to test his control. He would experiment. "Everyone stand." They all did. All was well.

"Everybody spread your arms." Confusion. Eliminate that in the future.

"Touch your toes." They all did. Going great.

"Squat." Everyone to a person was following his directions. He smiled at his power. Just then he dropped his watch.

"Oh shit," he said as he stooped over to pick up his watch. It took as week to clean up the theater.

THE SECRET TO LIFE

ONCE IN A WHILE the priest would get philosophical. Like when he read this tale about LIFE. Man comes into the world without his consent and leaves against his will. During his stay on earth, his time is spent in one continual round of hostilities and diagreements. When he's a baby, he's an angel. When he is a boy, he's a devil, and when he's a man he is everything from a skunk on up. In his duties, he is a fool. If he raises a family, he is a chump; if he bounces a check, the law turns around and raises hell with him.

If he is a poor man, he is a poor manager and has no sense; if he is rich he is dishonest, but considered smart. If he is in politics, he is a grafter and a crook; if he is out of politics, you can't place him because he is an undesirable citizen. If he goes to church, he is a hypocrite; if he stays away from church, he is a sinner. If he donates to foreign missions, he does it for show; if he does not, he is stingy and tightfisted. When he comes into the world, everybody wants to kiss him; when he goes out, everyone wants to kick him. If he dies young, there was a great future before him, but if he lives to a ripe old age, he is in the way, only living to save funeral expenses. LIFE IS A FUNNY ROAD, BUT WE ALL LIKE TO TRAVEL IT JUST THE SAME.

ANOTHER VIEWPOINT

Ernie had an entirely different outlook on life, and thought he could summarize it much better with this little limerick he had composed:

> When I'm in a somber mood
> I worry, work, and think.
> And when I'm in a drunken mood
> I frolic, play, and drink.
> But when my rambling days are over
> And my time has come to pass
> I hope they bury me upside down
> So the world can kiss my ass.

YOU'RE THE ONLY ONE FOR ME

This happily married couple were having dinner in a posh restaurant one evening, when the wife asked her husband, "If I died, you don't have anybody in mind to give my clothes, do you?" He answered, "Of course not."

"My jewelry?"

"Why, no!!"

"My most importasnt possession, my golf clubs. You wouldn't give them to another woman, would you?"

"No. Besides that, she's left-handed!"

FIRST THINGS FIRST

The know-it-all's time was overdue. He told about Ole, the Swedish Ski Champion, who had been called up for active duty in the Ski Patrol without warning. Knowing he would be gone for a few years, Ole married his sweetheart, and immediately left for duty in the ski patrol. Their assignment was to foil attempted border crossings.

After serving his government with distinction for five years, he finally was discharged and arrived at his home. He was a favorite for the press corps. They interviewed him the very next day, for they were inquisitive as to whether he would pursue his brilliant career. One of the reporters apologized for interrupting he and his bride, after they had been separated for such a long time.

The reporter said, "We know you have been apart for lo these five years, and we are indeed sorry to bother you." He chuckled as he went on, " We know what you and your beautiful bride did when you arrived home, but tell us, what was the second thing you did?"

Ole answered them matter of factly, "I took off my skis."

BOWLING NIGHT

The widow was smirking and patiently waiting her turn to tell about the two guys who worked side by side and one of them asked his buddy if he wanted to go bowling that night. "I'd sure like to," he said, "but it isn't worth it. My wife doesn't understand that bowling takes time and she always beats up on me for coming home late."

"I suppose you make the same mistake that most guys do, when they arrive home a little late. Tell me just what happens when you get home," his partner asked.

"The last time I went out was about a month ago. The first thing I did when I came down the street, I turned off the headlights, shut the motor off, and glided into the driveway. Then I snuck in through the front door, and closed it without making a sound. I very carefully took off my shoes in the foyer in order to not make any noise, and started for the bedroom. I no more than got out of the foyer and, whammo, she hit me with the rolling pin. I tell you, it's just not worth it."

"You're going about it all wrong."

"What do you do?"

"The first thing I do when I come down the street, is turn the headlights up to bright. Then when I come into the driveway, I rev up the motor two or three times, so my wife is sure to hear me. When I come in the front door, I slam it real hard. When I take off my shoes, I hold them up and drop them on the floor one at a time. Then I whistle a fast tune, and go into the bedroom. I take off my clothes, and put on my pajamas. Next I slap her on the fanny and asked her, "How about taking one tonight, dear? Nine times out of ten, she pretends she's asleep."

YOU CAN NOT BEAT EDUCATION

THE IRISH BACHELOR, an uneducated man, thought this story was unusually funny. One evening, two men entered a motel to secure accomodations for the night. When the clerk offered the registration form to one of the men for his signature, he signed it with an " X ".

Somewhat flustered, the clerk asked the gentleman if that X meant what he thought it did.

"Oh yes," said the young man. "That's my name, all right."

The clerk thought this over for a minute, and then asked the second gentleman if he would consent signing for the room.

"No problem," said the young man, whereupon he signed for the room with a double X, like so - X X.

"Now I presume," said the clerk, "that the first " X " means that's your name. But what is the second " X " for?"

"I've got a P.H.D."

PASSING GAS

Just as the crowd had tapered off in their laughter at the last joke, an elderly man in the audience, who was seated on a plank thrown across two barrels, evidently figured he could pass some gas without anybody noticing. But the seat reverberated like a big bass drum, causing an uproar. The Belgian farmer likened it to someone who tries to slip a calf under a fence and a bull comes roaring through. Flatulence has plagued mankind in all of history, is a natural release of the production of gases in the intestines, but is still considered vulgar by many people. However, it produces some of the best gags. This man's release set off a whole line of jokes about gas; the Belgian farmer started them off.

DOCTOR, THEY DON'T STINK!!!

The old Belgian farmer said, "You know it's awfully hard to control yourself at times. Like this young feller that had a particularly difficult time with indigestion causing him much pain and a continuous tendency to farting. He would fart at the most inconvenient times. It was so severe, that he lost one job after another and he finally admitted to himself that he needed professional help.

He made an appointment with a physician, and on his first visit, he told the doctor his problem, but added, "Luckily, they don't stink." So the doctor gave him a prescription to aid his digestion and the man left. "I want to see you in another week," said the doctor.

The next week the man came back, told the doctor he had followed his instructions as to taking the medication, but the farting continued. Again he added, "Luckily, they don't stink," cutting a few while he was being examined. The doctor raised his eyebrows, and said, "We'll have to try something else." He gave him another prescription, and made an appointment to see him again in a week.

In another week, the man returned. "The prescription didn't work, but it's still the same, "I fart a lot, but thankfully, they don't stink."

The doctor said, "Get up on my table here and lie down. I want to give you a thorough exam." He then turned around facing the patient with his lamp and mirror on his forehead. The man was perplexed. "What are you doing?" he asked. "My trouble is not in my head; you're looking at the wrong end."

The doctor replied, "I'm going to operate on your nose, you stinking S.O.B.."

ADD THE GAS

A lady went to a sports store to pick up a gift for her husband's birthday. As she shopped, she decided that she would get him some fishing equipment, but when she priced a rod and reel, it added up to more money than she had with her; the items she had selected came to $50.00 and all she had with her was $35.00 . She didn't want to disappoint her husband, for his birthday was the very next day. She didn't have enough time to go home and come back before the store closed for the weekend, so she stuffed the reel into her blouse, vowing that she would return to pay for it when the store re-opened again on Monday. She proceeded to the counter to check out the rod.

Being somewhat nervous about her dishonesty, she fumbled her purse and dropped her wallet .As she placed the rod on the counter and bent over to pick up her wallet., the reel rolled out of her blouse, and she inadvertently passed some gas.

The clerk added up the purchases saying, "That comes to $55.,'mam' ."

"How do you arrive at $55., isn't that supposed to be $50.?"

"$35. for the rod, the reel is $15, and $5 for the duck call."

ANNIE, GET YOUR GUN

Ernie was reminded of this true-to-life tale about a rather large woman who entered the public bus in Milwaukee for a ride home. She was laden down with two large bags of groceries. She had trouble trying to find the correct coins in her purse and balancing the groceries on her arm at the same time. Before she could insert the coins in the slot, the strain of the shuffling caused one of the bags to break and oranges started cascading down the aisle. As she tried to retrieve them, each time she stooped over, she passed some gas.

The bus driver observed all this and couldn't resist commenting, "That's right, lady. If you can't catch'em, shoot'em."

- 120 -

WE NEED A NEW TOILET, GRANDPA

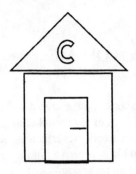

The Belgian farmer had to be excused for telling stories from another generation, but the crowd welcomed his contributions, as they were stories they just had never heard before. A good joke always remains a good joke no matter when it is told. He started out by explaining that this tale is based on the times before the days of indoor toilet facilities when everybody used outdoor toilets.

Every spring someone was assigned the unenviable task of cleaning the outdoor privy. This was truly a terrible and degrading task. Nobody volunteered; the father simply said, "This year, son, it's your turn. Get it done before two weeks go by, OK?"

Since he had never done this before, he spent considerable time analyzing how it could be accomplished without getting his hands dirty. There just had to be a better way than hand labor. He questioned all in the household before it finally dawned on him, "Why not blow it out of the hole?"

He bought a stick of dynamite, and early one fine morning when everybody in the house was still asleep, he attached a fuse, put the dynamite down the hole of the outdoor toilet, and strung the fuse out a safe distance.

While he rolled out the fuse, with his back to the house, he was unaware that Grandpappy had arisen mighty early also, had an undeniable urge, and with one hand on his pajamas was speeding toward the toilet. The young fellow lit the fuse and waited for results.

There was a tremendous BOOM, and everything went flying in the air. The toilet was blown completely apart, the contents spread all over the back yard, and Grandpappy ended up in a tree.

As he hung by a limb, he surveyed the damage and exclaimed, "Boy, am I glad I didn't leave <u>that one</u> in the house!!!"

PLAY A TUNE FOR ME

THE WIDOW wanted to shake up the crowd so she told about this doctor who had such an over scheduled number of patients that he was at his wit's end. Nevertheless, he couldn't turn any of them downand kept receiving more and more patients, even walk-ins that had no appointment, stacking them up in every room he had.

One man had a particular problem that he was hesitant to discuss. He said, "Doctor, I have an uncontrollable desire to sing while I'm having sex."

The doctor listened, but had no immediate remedy. He said, "Go to the last room down the hall,and wait for me. It's going to be a while." He needed to do a little research before he could treat such a problem. Then he went back to his other patients. He was so busy that he soon forgot he had even seen the man.

About six patients later, a woman came in with a similar problem to the man he had seen earlier, the difference being that she had an urge to pass gas every time she had intercourse. He told her to go down to the last room down the hall and wait until he could see her.

When he had seen his last patient for the day, he suddenly remembered the man and woman he had sent down the hall to wait in the room there. "Oh, my God," he said. "How could I forget those two people?"

As he hurried down the hall, visions of Joe, the accordian player, came to his mind, for this is what he heard. A man singing, "Hold that tiii-ger, and a woman answering with a big bruuu-up. Hold that tiii-ger, bruuu-up."

The widow had the crowd roaring, so she went on
with this pretty little Christmas poem:

THAT LITTLE FUR CAP

The next night was Christmas, the night it was still
The stockings were hung by the chimney to fill;
Nothing was stirring at all in the house,
For fear that St. Nicholas would not come to our
house.

The children were dried and gone to their bed,
And Mother in her night gown and I on ahead
Were searching around in the closet for toys.
We crept around quiet, not to raise any noise.

Now Mother was carrying all the toys in her gown
Showing her person from her waist on down
When we came near the crib of our little boy
Our youngest and sweetest, our pride and our joy.

He opened his eyes wide, as he peeked from his cot,
And he seed everything, his mother has got.
But he didn't even notice the toys in her lap,
He just asked, "For who's that little fur cap?"

"Hush," Mother said, as she laughed with delight,
"I think I'll give that, to your Father tonight."

FRED SCHMITT

The last laugh belonged to Billy Bugger. He had been quiet all night saving up this tale. He said, "He who laughs last, laughs best." See what you think when you get through with this tale about a campaign rally that was being held in a large hall for the candidate, Fred Schmitt, who was up for reelection for Mayor of the city. The campaign manager was a good talker and promoter for his candidate. He explained to the crowd why they should reelect Fred Schmitt. He began in the usual fashion, pretending that the Mayor actually gave them something, "Who is the man that got the federal grant for the beautiful park down by the river?"

And all the people, led by some of the party's plants in the audience, replied in unison, "Fred Schmitt." But there was one little guy in the back of the audience who yelled, "Fred Schmitt is a dumb shit."

The campaign manager ignored him and asked the audience, "Who is the man that forced the governor to give more money to our fair city?" Again the crowd answered in a loud voice, "Fred schmitt." And again the little guy called out, "Fred Schmitt is a dumb shit."

The campaign manager was trying to ignore him, so he asked the audience this question, "Who was the man that hired more women and minorities than anybody else in this city?" And the crowd dutifully cried out, "Fred Schmitt." But the little guy in the back of the hall persisted. He said, "Fred Schmitt is a dumb shit."

The campaign manager now knew that he could no longer ignore the little guy, so he tried a different tactic. He would embarass and intimidate him. Most people don't like to talk to large groups and are actually afraid to do so, so the campaign manager pointed to his adversary, and said, "Will the man who keeps referring to Fred Schmitt in such an uncomplimentary manner, please come up to the stage, take the microphone, and explain to the audience why he thinks so unfavorably of Fred Schmitt."

This had worked many times in the past for the campaign manager when he encountered hecklers. Normally, the agitator would slide down in his seat, refuse to take up the challenge, and not be heard from again for the rest of the evening. But lo and behold, the short man who was very muscular, had a very distinctive swagger, which Billy enacted out to the crowd's delight, came strutting up to the stage, grabbed the microphone, and said, "I'll tell you why Fred Schmitt is a dumb shit."

"Five years ago, I had a farm with all fine cattle on it. I also had a prize winning bull that was worth thousands of dollars. But he got sick on me, so I called the veterinarian to get his advice. He looked over my bull and said he was constipated. ' He needs immediate treatment,' he told me. So I asked how to treat him, and he said I should give the bull an enema. I asked how do you give a bull an enema, and he said, 'I only give the advice; how you give the bull an enema is your problem.' "

The campaign manager interrupted him. "What has this to do with Fred Schmitt?"

"Just hold your horses," said the burly little man. "I'm coming to that. I sat up half the night trying to figure out how to give a bull an enema. Finally an idea came to my head. My father used to play the french horn, and I knew it was still up in the attic. So I got a flashlight, crawled up there, and sure enough it was there. So I took it down, and mixed up some soap suds. I made a nice batch of suds with lots of bubbles."

The campaign manager was impatient.
"You are telling us a long story, but what in the world does all
this have to do with my candidate, Fred Schmitt?"

"Now, just a minute, just a minute. I'm coming to
that. I go out in the barn with my french horn and the soap
suds, and I hang a burlap bag over the window. After all, it
would look funny if somebody saw me at the back of the bull
with a french horn. All the while the bull is eyeing me up and
down, but I thought he was pretty well tied in his stanchion
even though I didn't think he would like what I was going to
do to him. So I took the french horn and rammed it into his
rear to start the enema. I was right; he didn't like it. He
reared up on his hind legs, and busted out with the stanchion
around his neck. Down the road he went with the french horn
sticking out of his rear end."

The campaign manager just couldn't contain himself
any longer. "Will you please get to the point and tell us, for
goodness sakes, how Fred Schmitt enters into this!!"

"You bet, now I'm going to tell you. Fred Schmitt
was the bridge tender that day. And just as my prize bull came
to the bridge, Fred Schmitt opened it, and my prize bull fell
into the river and drowned. And I still say Fred Schmitt is a
dumb shit. Because anybody, that can't tell the difference between a tug boat whistle, and a bull farting through a french
horn, is a dumb shit!!!"